WATERS
OF
REFLECTION

WATERS OF REFLECTION

Meditations for every day

SANDRA DRESCHER-LEHMAN

Good Books
Intercourse, PA 17534

Photo Credits

Front cover: R. Markham-Smith; Jess Lopatynski—47, 109;
© W. L. McCoy—7, 18, 31, 58, 122, 136, 146; © Dwain Patton—90,
160; Dawn J. Ranck—77.

Design by Dawn J. Ranck

WATERS OF REFLECTION: MEDITATIONS FOR EVERY DAY
Copyright © 1993 by Good Books, Intercourse, Pennsylvania 17534
International Standard Book Number: 1-56148-084-3
Library of Congress Catalog Card Number: 93-1433

Library of Congress Cataloging-in-Publication Data

Drescher-Lehman, Sandra.
    Waters of reflection : meditations for every day / Sandra Drescher-Lehman.
        p.   cm.
    ISBN 1-56148-084-3 (pkb.) : $8.95
    1. Devotional calendars. I. Title.
BV4811.D67 1993
242'.2—dc20
                                                                                93-1433
                                                                                CIP

To John,
my husband and best friend,
who has helped me know many faces of God—
especially of unconditional love.

Table of Contents

Introduction

Water, for a long time, has been a powerful symbol of God's presence in my life. For that reason, reading Scriptures which include the theme or suggestion of water has become a meaningful way for me to relate to God.

In the following pages, I have chosen daily Scriptures which speak of some of the many attributes of God. I have brought them together under various themes of water, which exemplify the nature of these attributes. Each day's Scripture and suggested responses are brief, but can take as much time as you have to give. My hope for these meditational readings and exercises is that, through them, God will become more real to you, that you will become more like Jesus Christ, and that you can learn to live more and more of your moments in the conscious power of the Holy Spirit within you.

I've found it most helpful to have my daily times with the Shepherd at a regular time. When I schedule it into my day like any other appointment, it becomes an occasion I look forward to. I don't always feel like it—feelings do go up and down—but it has become part of my commitment to my growing relationship with my Friend and Guide.

I have found it helpful to set a predetermined length of time that I expect to spend alone with God. If I do it while waiting for a phone call or if I try to squeeze it between other duties as quickly as possible, the benefits I receive are limited. I can speak and listen more freely when I don't harbor the option of finishing early.

You may want to claim your own special place of prayer. It may be a certain room or a chair. It may be a corner in a library or a tree outside. It is only important that it is your special undisturbed place where you can expect to meet the Great Provider. As you meet with God repeatedly in the same place, your expectations will grow for your times together. Your memories of good times together will draw you back and also sustain you in the dry times. You will remember and know God is present, even when your feelings aren't sure.

When you get to your special place of prayer, at your set hour for a specific length of time, first spend time becoming quiet. Relax, close your eyes to outer stimuli, and become thankfully aware of your total dependence on your Powerful and Merciful God. You may want to spend your entire time relaxing in these Arms of Love.

As you become ready for further direction, read the suggested Scripture of the day. I deliberately chose short passages, intending them to be devotional, rather than study, material (although there is certainly a place for Bible study in our lives as well). Read the passage slowly and prayerfully, stopping when a word or phrase speaks to you, and pondering it in your heart. Ask your Leader to speak to you, and take time to listen for the Lord's response. It is not important that you finish reading the entire passage; only that you respond to what the Almighty has for you for that day of your life.

If you want ideas for how to make the Word of God more meaningful, go on to read the suggestion which follows. Use what makes sense to you, but don't let it limit you. Let it be only a starting point!

As you close your time of prayer, ask God to help you take the knowledge of God's presence, Jesus' example, and the Spirit's power into the rest of your life as well. Your set times with God should remind and enable you to make every minute of every day a prayer.

We are each individual persons, and we each have a unique way of relating to our Omnipresent God. Some of us think about the only Wise God primarily in intellectual terms. Others of us relate more easily on the level of our feelings. Some pray best in writing. Some persons' prayers lie in the activity of their days.

I designed these scriptural exercises with a variety of ideas for these many different personalities. You will undoubtedly find some days' suggestions more fitting for you to follow than others. You will discover that you need extra energy to pray in a way that is not your first nature. Your relationship with your Awe-inspiring God will grow, however, if you are willing to learn and practice new ways of praying.

In my study and planning, I used the New International Version (NIV) of the Bible. It may be helpful for you to use that version as well, especially to find the same examples of water images that I use.

My prayer is that there is much more in store for you in these pages than I have written. It will come to you in a particular way as the Mighty One blesses your meditation and love. May our Glorious Creator enrich your life as you nurture this growing relationship and expand your knowledge of who God is.

—Sandra Drescher-Lehman

GOD
of the
Ice and
Snow

Majestic

A new year opens in majesty! It stretches out before us, pregnant with possibilities and endless with expectations. And God, the epitome of majesty, reigns over all of it—past, present, and future, in perfect grandeur.

If I were to put an image to the sense of majesty that accompanies this new year's adventure in living, I would choose the glorious mountains of ice and snow in the Arctic and in Antarctica. They explode with beauty from their mammoth hidden foundations and are vivid witnesses to the wondrous majesty of the God who created them.

Another beautiful symbol of God's majesty is much smaller and much nearer: the icicles that form when the snow begins to melt, when the water trickles off the roof, down the side of a fence or around the rocks in the river. In the glistening sun of winter, they sparkle and, in miniature, they hold the wonder and magnificence of the grand glaciers!

As we begin this new year of our lives, let us meditate on the majesty of God. Our God is beyond comparison, even to the most majestic thing our human minds can comprehend—the mountainous ice masses of the land to the far north and south, or the long icicles that we see in our own neighborhoods. As Creator of everything we have ever seen or heard about, God and God's majesty are above and beyond our wildest imaginations.

Just as we believe in the majestic beauty of the earth whether or not we have actually seen it, we can also believe in the reality of God's majesty, whether or not we can perceive it. "Oh Lord, our Lord, how majestic is your name in all the earth!"

JANUARY 1 — Read Psalm 8

Look around you in the newness and freshness of the first day of a new year. Where do you find God's majestic name in all the earth you see today? Add your praise to the lines of Psalm 8.

JANUARY 2 — Read Isaiah 55:6-13

Take a walk in the beauty of God's world and seek the Lord. Go out in joy and be led forth in peace. Join the earth, bursting into song, and the trees clapping their hands! If your world has snow or icicles, take time to really see in them the grandeur and majesty of God.

JANUARY 3 — Read II Peter 1:16-18

Imagine yourself with Peter and Jesus on the sacred mountain when they hear the voice from the Majestic Glory saying, "This is my Son, whom I love; with him I am well pleased." Sit quietly, letting the majesty of God and the glory of Jesus fill your mind. Let the Spirit fill your heart with love and awe.

JANUARY 4 — Read Exodus 15:1-6

Let the song of Moses also be your prayer. After verse 5, add the miracles of God which you have witnessed in the past year.

JANUARY 5   Read Jude 24, 25

Dedicate yourself anew today to God's majesty, glory, power, and authority, through Jesus Christ our Lord. Rest for a few minutes in the knowledge that you are a great joy to your Savior.

JANUARY 6   Read Job 37:14-24

Stop with Job to consider God's wonders which have reminded you of God's majesty this week. Hold a piece of ice in your hand and feel it melt. Experience this miracle of water transformation as one of God's wonders.

JANUARY 7   Read Hebrews 1

The earth, which contains much evidence of God's majesty, will eventually perish. God's majesty shown in Jesus is what will remain. Let the snow, ice, mountains, trees, water, and sky be reminders today of their Creator and of your personal friendship with your Majesty.

Powerful

A few months ago, winter came earlier than usual to our part of the country. We were still enjoying the crisp air of fall and the beauty of its turning leaves when we were suddenly interrupted by an unexpected snowstorm.

It came slowly at first, but as the flakes continued to pile up, one by one, the light delicate crystals combined into powerful mounds of heavy snow. Each leaf acted as a cupped hand for the snow, and branches began to break under the weight of the accumulation. The innocent looking white fluff had quickly become a great source of power.

I understand that the roofs on houses in some northern areas, where they receive a lot of snow each year, are built at a steep slant to prevent the accumulation of this powerful weight. The snow is more likely to slide off, rather than build up enough to damage the structure. Even so, residents often have to help further by shoveling the snow off their roofs.

God is gentle like the snow that falls, one flake at a time. God comes to us quietly, almost imperceptibly at times. But God can also unleash power and change the world.

Snow can bring an entire area to a halt. We change our plans, cancel our meetings, and give in to sitting still and watching the snow. Whether or not we enjoy its power and see its beauty is our choice.

God, too, comes to us constantly and persistently in love. We can put up steep roofs over our lives to resist the accumulation of God's power and beauty. Or we can let the refreshment of God's love pile up around us and change our plans. We can enjoy the fresh excitement of what our lives can grow into when we acknowledge and worship our God of power.

JANUARY 8   Read Psalm 18:16-29

When you begin to feel snowed under this week, remember these verses and know that you don't have to be powerful enough to handle it all alone. God is more powerful than your most powerful enemy, whether it's a person, your schedule, or a task. Take care of your own faithfulness, purity, and humility, and trust God to provide the power.

JANUARY 9   Read Job 37:1-13

Be still and remember the ways you've witnessed the unleashing of God's mighty power recently. Then remember the ways in which this same God has also come to you personally, in the quiet power of love, just for you. Let those two extremes on the continuum of power melt together in your heart as you worship.

JANUARY 10   Read Exodus 9:13-35

When have you, like Pharaoh, hardened your heart to the fear of God, even in the midst of obvious signs of God's power? Make a list, as you go through the day, of where you see God's power at work in the world, in your church, in those you meet, and within yourself. We, too, deserve to be hailed upon, but, thank God, we are loved instead.

JANUARY 11   Read Ephesians 6:10-18

Not only do we worship a God of power, but we also are called to be strong in the Lord and are given the means with which to do it. Draw a picture of yourself, protected by the armor of God. How does each piece affect your life?

JANUARY 12   Read Proverbs 25:13

Are you refreshing to the Spirit of God who sends you into the world? Pray that you will also be a refreshing sign of God's power to those your life touches today, as the first snowfall of the season invigorates those who eagerly await it.

JANUARY 13   Read Psalm 147:12-20

Exchange the name of your town or city with "Jerusalem" and the name of your family with "Zion" in verse 12. Then pray that you will live to see God's power and blessings as revealed in these verses. Close, as this Psalm does, in praise of the Lord.

JANUARY 14   Read Isaiah 40:6-26

For your meditation today, fill a clear glass with ice cubes and set it before you. Watch the ice melt, symbolizing God's power (in the hardness of the ice), as well as God's gentle shepherding (in the melting). God, in power, is far above us in comparison, and yet God also comes down to us, in love, in Jesus. Thank God for combining both extremes into the Friend you have by your side, who watches the ice melt with you.

❧

Merciful

When I was a child, one of my favorite winter activities was building igloos. I treasured the experience especially because I could do it so rarely. The conditions had to be just right—we needed six to twelve inches of heavy snow that would pack together perfectly. We cut the snow into blocks with a shovel and piled them on top of each other to make the walls. Then my tallest brother carefully built the layers inward until the edges met in a domed roof. I felt like I was jumping right into pictures I'd seen of Eskimo igloos.

What was most amazing and intriguing about our snow huts, though, was that they were actually warm inside! In the center of solid snow and ice, surrounded by the coldest building material imaginable, we were warm enough to take off our coats and have a winter picnic! The promise of the warm ending carried us through the cold process of getting there.

As I look back at some of my experiences since those childhood projects, I see how much God's mercy is like the warmth of our snow huts. Those times when I have been most exposed to the cold or the cutting winds of grief or my own sinfulness have also provided the best conditions for me to feel God's warmth of mercy.

As long as everything in my life is skipping along easily and happily, I have little reason to think about the mercy of God. It is when the going is choppy and hard and sad that I suddenly find myself crying out in need. And God has always been right there, just waiting for me to accept the love and forgiveness that only God can give.

Adversity in life comes to everyone. Whether or not we grow from those times depends on what we do with them. If we try to run from our problems in bitterness, we will likely remain cold. If we accept God's warm igloo of mercy, however, we can find relief in the middle of our troubles, and even because of them!

Our God is full of mercy, looking for people who will receive it.

JANUARY 15   **Read Psalm 51**

Draw a picture in your journal of a clean white igloo. Around it, draw the things in your life from which you want to be cleansed. Inside, indicate God's mercy. Finally place yourself in the space where you are presently living. If you are living closer to one of the outside sins, try to move inside the igloo to accept the warmth of God's mercy. What will that require?

JANUARY 16   **Read Isaiah 1:16-20**

Black is the absence of color. White is a combination of all the colors. What do you need to have added to the array of color in your life to make your sins as white as snow? Your Merciful God would like to add it.

JANUARY 17   Read Psalm 106

A Psalm of mercy! God forgives the children of Israel over and over again. Write a letter of thanks to God for all the times you have fallen away and have known God's mercy extended to bring you back.

JANUARY 18   Read Matthew 20:29-34

Make this Scripture your personal prayer: "Lord, Son of David, have mercy on me." Say it over and over until it becomes as regular and natural as your breathing. Imagine Jesus' compassion and mercy coming to you as snow falling until you are surrounded by the warmth of your igloo.

JANUARY 19   Read Zechariah 7:8-10

Offer a prayer today in praise of God's mercy in your life. Then ask for God's help in turning every potential thought of evil into one of mercy and compassion.

JANUARY 20   Read Micah 6:6-8

Because God is merciful to us, we are also required to be merciful to others—in justice, love, and humility. Plan an act of mercy in Christ's name today. Then do it!

JANUARY 21   Read Matthew 5:7

Have you received Christ's blessing because of the mercy you've shown to others this week? Sometimes when we think we are only giving, we realize that we also have much to receive. Begin by relaxing and letting the promise of this verse wrap itself around you as a gently falling blanket of snow. Enjoy His mercy.

GOD
of the
Springs

Living Word

*R*iding our bicycles down the coast of California, John, my husband, and I often stopped to get a drink at one of the many roadside springs. They were marked on our bikers' maps, which we consulted often, and were indeed a bikers' oasis. We were carrying pint-sized plastic bottles of water fastened onto the frames of our bikes, but it was never long before the water had warmed up to the temperature around us. The cold springs were definitely a treat! We often met other bikers at those spots of refreshment, where they, too, were enjoying the never-ending water. That trip was six years ago, yet I know that ice-cold water continues to burst from the ground at those same places today.

Last summer I visited a camp where my parents had taken pictures of me as a two-year-old, drinking from a spring. The water was still bubbling.

I'm sure the springs on the farm where I grew up are still the home of crayfish, a feeding trough for animals, and an occasional playground for children. Close to the house on that farm was a well which held a similar mystery for me. It was a big hole in the ground whose supply of water provided our family with all the drinks and washing we needed or wanted, and we never had to work to replenish it!

No wonder images of springs and fountains and wells are often used to describe God! Not only does God provide a refreshing oasis when we find ourselves heated or in trouble, but we are also promised the miracle that our God is always there. Even when we walk away from the Source of Life, we are always invited and welcomed back. We do not worship a God of the past alone, but a Living God who is continuously with us on each of our unique journeys. Blessed be God forever!

JANUARY 22   Read Psalm 36:7-10

Eat, drink, and find your refuge and peace in God's love! It was not only available for the Psalmist, but the Living God continues to bubble forth, ready to enrich your life. Let this fountain live within you today.

JANUARY 23   Read John 4:4-26

Imagine Jesus telling this story to you Himself. Let yourself be the woman, replacing "Samaritan woman" with the name by which you are called. What sin does Jesus talk to you about? What is the form of living water the Messiah has for you? Drink together.

JANUARY 24   Read Jeremiah 2:13-17

Walking away from God elicits a second sin—insisting on doing things my own way. Ask Jesus' forgiveness for the times you have let your broken cisterns replace the spring of living water He has made available for you. Close your time of prayer with the promise and confession of Jeremiah 3:12, 13.

JANUARY 25   Read Revelation 21:6, 7

Revelation was written as a loving word of hope to a persecuted people. How is this promise of a free drink, from the spring of the water of life, good news to you today? Ask the Holy Spirit to help you compose a letter of thanks to the Alpha and the Omega.

JANUARY 26   **Read Isaiah 12**

What does the "well of salvation" offer to you personally? Name three to five glorious things the Holy One has done for you. Imagine that you are a spring of living water, proclaiming as you bubble forth into your world (quietly or with shouting), the exultation of God!

JANUARY 27   **Read I Thessalonians 1:2-10**

Who comes to your mind as you pray verses 2 and 3? Bring life to the Living Word by letting that person or persons know how much you thank God for their work produced by faith, their labor prompted by love, and their endurance inspired by hope.

JANUARY 28   **Read Proverbs 14:27**

Memorize this verse, changing "a man" to "me." Take it into your day as the Living Word of promise—the Lord calls you away from death, to life!

Gracious

Wsen we visited some friends in Guatemala a couple of years ago, we were able to go with them into the villages where they frequently traveled as health workers. We saw a beautiful mountainous land inhabited by a gracious people. We saw the flat, rich land claimed by wealthy landowners for coffee and banana plantations, and the steep mountainsides, left for the poor Guatemalan Indians. In fact, some of their fields were so steep that farmers had been killed by falling out of their cornfields.

One Sunday we hiked up one of the steep mountain trails. Along the way we met many men and women going down with empty jars or returning with water from the river, miles below. When our guide sensed my amazement at the time and energy it took to obtain water, he asked, "How do you draw water in your town?"

I thought back to the small farm where I grew up. I remember learning that our water came from the well beside our porch, but I had never seen how it got into the house.

I suddenly realized that I am part of the minority of people in the world who put little energy into getting the water they use. And it is through no virtue of my own that I learned the hot from the cold spigot rather than the trail to the closest well or river.

God's grace comes to me much like the well water of my childhood—unexplainable, unearned, and undeserved. God is not gracious because of who I am, but because of the sinner I am. Through Christ's death and resurrection, God is gracious—giving freely.

I don't deserve the well beside my house while many people in the world have to walk miles for water, but I enjoy its water. I also don't deserve the grace that God, through Jesus, has made available for me. Lord, help me to continue drinking from your well without trying to earn your grace.

JANUARY 29   Read Psalm 25

In what verse are you reminded of the grace of God in your own
life? Stop at that phrase or word and give God thanks for that
undeserved act of love and forgiveness which you have received.

JANUARY 30   Read Zechariah 12:10 to 13:2

Think of a time when you have rejected God's grace and thereby
participated in piercing Jesus. Spend time in mourning and
repentance. Then imagine God's forgiveness erupting like a
fountain from the well of grace, cleansing you from sin and
impurity.

JANUARY 31   Read II Peter 3:14-18

Pray for help in this challenge from Peter to make every effort to
be found spotless, blameless, and at peace with God. When you
remember the times you fall short, be thankful that God's grace
has covered that part of your life.

FEBRUARY 1   Read Isaiah 30:19-21

List the idols you hang onto that keep you from being the person
God is calling you to be. "How gracious he will be when you cry
for help!" (v. 19) Can you accept God's help without having to
earn it?

FEBRUARY 2   Read I Peter 1:13-21

Does this call to holiness seem an impossible task? Draw a picture of a well in your journal and fill it with all the gifts Jesus gave you freely in His death by choice. Journal about how your life is different because you "drink from this well."

FEBRUARY 3   Read Psalm 119:25-32

Do you think of laws as keeping you from having fun or as protecting you? How does your answer to that correspond with how you understand God's law and God's grace? Notice how the Psalmist combines them!

FEBRUARY 4   Read Revelation 22:21

Ask your Gracious God to bring people to your mind for prayer. Then pray this benediction for each person who comes into your consciousness for the next ten or twenty minutes. Resolve to pray this verse for others you see and think of throughout the day.

Guide

*C*rabtree Falls in the mountains of western Virginia is one of my favorite getaway spots. I park at the bottom of the Falls, then hike three miles to the top. Every step is worth the effort. All along the way is one spectacular sight after another, as the river cascades over rocks and through the air, breaking up the huge falls into many separate displays of splendor.

A huge rock proclaims "Welcome to the Top," as it stretches out on both sides of the spring-fed river and watches the water prepare for its first descent. From that vantage point one can also see the mountains, roads, and trees for miles around. The air is clear, the sunshine brighter, and no foliage blocks the view. I let my mind drift off with the infinity of sky and earth, intrigued by the fact that among all its options, the river knows exactly where to go. Over the years, its map has been worn into the hard rocks, so that from the moment the water bubbles from the earth, it knows the direction to follow.

When I get to the top of a mountain in life where I can see many options, I tend to hop excitedly between many places. Even though God has gone ahead as my Guide, carving out my path, I don't flow into it as naturally as the spring becomes the waterfalls.

I can't imagine beauty in a fall, so I look for an easier path. I am ready to follow my Guide as long as it appears to be the most fun way to go! But it is when I can take the risk of following, even when it looks like I am giving up everything, that my life has the potential beauty of a waterfall. Its magnificence is in its falling.

A stream seems to tumble over the ledge of a mountain so naturally. Lord, help me to trust Your guidance just as naturally and beautifully.

FEBRUARY 5   **Read Psalm 42:7-11**

Close your eyes and bring back to your mind the most beautiful waterfall you have ever seen. Let its roar drown out all the other noise around and within you. Rest quietly in the beauty and constancy of God, your Guide.

FEBRUARY 6   **Read Isaiah 58:6-11**

Needs in the world can be overwhelming. Rather than rushing out to obey the words in verses 6-10, meditate first on verse 11. Action needs to flow out of our own well-watered gardens to keep them from failing. Play soft music or enjoy the silence—whatever best nurtures your relationship of love with God today.

FEBRUARY 7   **Read John 13:1-17**

Yesterday you spent time loving God and letting God love you. Today let God direct your love to another. Plan an act of "foot-washing"—showing Jesus' love.

FEBRUARY 8   **Read Isaiah 49:8-10**

The children of Israel wanted to be restored, yet were afraid that God would not come to them. Is there a part of yourself which cannot trust God to guide you beside the refreshing springs of water? In your journal tell God your fears and ask for guidance through these struggles and doubts.

FEBRUARY 9   Read Luke 1:67-79

Sometimes, especially when we feel abandoned by God, it is helpful to be reminded of how active God has been in our personal history. Write your own "song" of praise, including times when you have known and seen God's guidance in your life.

FEBRUARY 10   Read Psalm 48

Dream big today. Ask God to guide your imagination and think of what you would yet like to do and who you would like to become in your lifetime. Close your prayer-dream with verse 14.

FEBRUARY 11   Read John 16:12-15

In today's prayer time, sip a glass or mug full of your favorite drink. As it goes down your throat, imagine the Holy Spirit guiding you as naturally and effortlessly in the direction you are to go. Pray that you will receive this guidance with humility and openness.

Pure

During my first experience on a weekend backpacking trip, I found myself on "water duty" as we prepared to set up camp on the first evening. Our hike leader told us to follow the stream we had been hiking along until we came to a spring he thought to be nearby. He said that the closer we got to the water's source, the more likely that the water would not be contaminated.

We were then to dip our containers in very slowly and carefully so as to not stir up the sediment on the bottom and muddy the water. The water downstream may have been safe to drink, too, but why should we have taken that chance when we could find pure water with just a little more effort?

That basic question continues to surface in my walk with God, as well. Why do I sometimes settle for what is likely okay, when I could be sure of my purity with just a little more effort? So often I live close to the edges, rather than in the center of God's will for me. I don't want to sin, but I want to get by with as much as possible. I know that God probably won't condemn me for the movie I'm watching, the music I'm listening to, the person I didn't help, or the way I'm spending my time. But I am also aware of ways in which I sometimes know God would be more positively glorified and ways I could be living more closely to the Source which energizes me.

After we found the spring and had filled three of our four containers on that camping trip, I got careless and dropped a canteen into the spring. Consequently, the last one was filled with dirty water. We boiled it later which made it safe to drink, but I felt badly about making extra work.

When I slip and muddy the purity of my walk with Christ, it is not impossible to "clear the water." Besides calling us to purity, God also forgives. But it's a waste of time and energy to step too close to the edges of God's will when I know where the center is.

FEBRUARY 12   Read Psalm 26

David, whose past sins are well known by all who read Scripture, shows complete confidence that he has been reinstated into purity with God. Pray for the gift of God's protection—to be kept in the center of God's pure and holy will.

FEBRUARY 13   Read Proverbs 25:26

How have you muddied the water in your life with wickedness? Ask Jesus how your well can be purified. Don't waste your time kicking yourself for past sins, but let God gently turn you in the right direction.

FEBRUARY 14   Read James 3:9-12

Spend time thinking about what there might be within you that adds bitterness to your life. Ask God to purify you so that you feel fresh inside like a mountain spring. Know, too, that pure words, thoughts, and actions will bubble out to those around you.

FEBRUARY 15   Read Psalm 119:9-16

What is one of the commands from God that you can "hide in your heart" today? Think of it as a spring within you—purifying your thoughts, motives, and actions. Repeat it over and over until it's as natural as your breathing. Pray that Christ will keep you reminded of His fresh presence throughout the day ahead.

FEBRUARY 16   **Read Matthew 5:8**

Only God is totally pure, and only in God, through Christ, can we be pure. Write a prayer of confession for the times this week when the impurity of your heart has kept you from seeing God clearly. Then receive Jesus' forgiveness and blessing to begin again.

FEBRUARY 17   **Read Proverbs 5:15-21**

Each life is like a deep well or never-ending spring, unable to be fully seen or known. Recognize the goodness God has given you in the friends you have. If you are married, write your spouse a reminder of your commitment or give a gift of love. If you are single, do the same for one of your best friends.

FEBRUARY 18   **Read Romans 16:19-20**

This letter was written by Paul "to all in Rome who are loved by God and called to be saints" (Romans 1:7). Would he brag about your obedience? The key to our purity lies in verse 20—the Lord's grace. Add your name to the end of verse 20 and receive these two verses as God's love letter to you.

GOD
of the
Rivers and
Streams

Strength

A t the end of a hot muggy day, I love to go down to the river, a mile away, to cool off. The place has something to offer for every mood!

Huge flat rocks on the banks and in the water provide great picnic spots. If I want to walk in solitude, I can hike to a point where the rocks are close enough together to jump all the way across to an island. One cove is especially good for fishing. Another is where the swimmers go.

Most of the time, though, I'm drawn to the rockiest area where the river's current is the strongest. Even though the water is only waist-deep there, it is a challenge to get from one rock to the next without being swept downstream.

On the most adventuresome sort of evening, I can find a niche among those rocks where I can strike a perfect balance, bracing my feet against a rock in front of me while letting my body lean back into the current for a great neck and back massage. I can actually let myself relax, knowing the waters' strength will hold me up.

It is that kind of balance that I think of when I meditate on the strength of God. I need to use the strength I've been given to get myself into the positions where God can use me. Unless I then lean into God's supporting strength, I will never know the thrill of being held by vitality beyond my own.

Take the risk, this week, of putting yourself in places where God can use you. Then, instead of listening to voices in society around you that tell you to "Be strong and stand on your own two feet," relax in the knowledge that God's strength shows up most clearly in your weakness.

FEBRUARY 19   Read Psalm 46

Practice verse 10. In stillness, know that God is God above all you know or imagine! In the safety of God's love, name your fears, doubts, and weaknesses. Imagine the river "whose streams make glad the city of God" holding you up. Invite God to be your strength all day.

FEBRUARY 20   Read Isaiah 32

Imagine the day that lies ahead as that of a barren desert—without plans or shape. Now imagine a stream of water flowing through your empty day, symbolizing God's willingness to fertilize the plans that will bring it to life. Trust, in your letting go of what no longer seems to be part of the day you had planned, that God will bring back what is really important.

FEBRUARY 21   Read Psalm 73:23-28

Stretch out your right hand for God to take hold of it. Read the rest of this Psalm out loud as your love letter to God.

FEBRUARY 22   Read Isaiah 43:1-7

Substitute your name for "Jacob" and "Israel" in verse 1. What are the waters and fire you are passing through? Believe that God's presence within you is your strength.

FEBRUARY 23   Read Ezekiel 29:1-6

Pharaoh thought he was God—that he owned the great river! In what similar way are you claiming to be God? Are you acting as if you own your money? Your time? Your friends? Your children? Live today so that it is evident to everyone who your Lord is.

FEBRUARY 24   Read Isaiah 40:28-31

Your times of weariness and weakness are not times to kick yourself. They are great chances to let God's strength shine through! Only in God's strength can you really fly.

FEBRUARY 25   Read Nehemiah 8:10, 11

Think of a song to sing that reveals the joy you find in living because God is your strength. Repeat it throughout the day as a reminder to yourself—this is a sacred day to the Lord.

Mother

*I*n my childhood home, my mother was always available. Dad went to work and sometimes was gone from home for days at a time, but I always knew Mother would be there.

I also knew that Mother would always tell me the truth. When my brothers and sister teased me, I knew Mother would protect me with her honesty. She did the other things expected of mothers too—she fed me, clothed me, loved me, read to me, prayed with me, and tucked me into bed each night.

Our earliest childhood memories have a lot to do with how we view the world. What a gift my mother has been to me, in helping my world view be one of love and security. Experiencing her love has also allowed me to more easily know God's love. God often comes to me as a Mother in whom I can totally put my trust.

It's the same feeling of trust I get as I lie in the bottom of a canoe, looking up into the starry moonlit sky while a friend paddles gently down the river. All I can hear of my friend's presence is the quiet dipping of the paddle in the water. And I know my friend's love so that I can trust him with my safety.

Sometimes all I knew of my mother's love was her quiet, ever-present spirit that proved trustworthy over and over again in my life.

All I know sometimes of God's love is the promise that it will always be there and the experiences that I have had which prove its truth.

FEBRUARY 26 {#february-26}
Read Psalm 131

Imagine yourself as a tiny baby, being held in the arms of your idea of the perfect mother. You have no words yet, only feelings— relaxed, trusting, loved. Stay with this imagery until you know God to be this ideal Mother to you.

FEBRUARY 27 {#february-27}
Read Isaiah 66:7-11

You didn't have a perfect mother. No one has. But God is with you to fill those holes of unfulfilled expectations. Write a letter to God explaining one of the hurts that you are reminded of when you think of your mother. How does God respond?

FEBRUARY 28 {#february-28}
Read Isaiah 66:12-14

What area of your life needs comforting? Let yourself imagine floating down a wide peaceful river in a canoe, lying on your back with God paddling. Listen to the sounds around you. Smell the river life. Tell God about your hurt feelings. Know that God really is listening and longs to comfort you.

FEBRUARY 29 {#february-29}
Read Matthew 23:37-39

Imagine yourself as a tiny chick, sitting alone by the barnyard stream. Your mother hen comes to envelop you under her wing.

Enjoy her warmth and comfort until you can affirm her representing your loving Lord. "Blessed are you who come in the name of the Lord."

MARCH 1   Read Isaiah 49:13-23

Each of us has received different levels of compassion from our mothers. God, however, has an equal and superior amount of love to give to each of us. Pray verse 13 in praise to God!

MARCH 2   Read Luke 15:8-10

Let the mother-heart of God be with you in everything you do and every place you go today. Begin with a prayer to be engulfed in God's love. When you catch yourself becoming lost to the awareness of God's presence, turn your attention back, in the joy of being found by God.

MARCH 3   Read Psalm 27

Listen to your heart which says, "Seek God's face." Look for God's face and character in the people you meet today. Take time to let the truth of verse 10 sink into the depths of your being, like a stream of refreshment.

MARCH 4　　　　　　　　　**Read Galatians 4:21-31**

You are a child of promise. God is your only perfect Mother. Make a list of the characteristics of a mother which God is providing in your life right now. Give thanks!

Leader

*A*s the sun peeped into the new day, my eyelids struggled to meet the light. My body said, "You're still tired; go back to sleep," but my mind slowly awakened to the reality of where I was. My friends and I were enjoying our first camping trip of the year. If I hurried, I could have time to myself before the others got up.

Sounds from the brook beckoned me to join its morning praise and I found myself eagerly heading for its banks. Perched on a rock by its edge, I soon became mesmerized by its gurgling rhythm.

As I watched and listened, I began to see my life in the life of the brook. The water was moving and yet it was always before me! Sometimes it went crashing into a rock and sprayed high into the air. Other times it flowed smoothly between the obstacles. Sometimes it came quietly into the pool beside my rock for a break. Other times it sped rapidly down the center of its bed. In the middle of its many patterns, however, the water kept up its continual flow.

I could see God's direction as I imagined a spring giving life to this brook somewhere up the mountain, and then the brook flowing into a river, making its way to the ocean and eventually evaporating into a cloud, ready to fall and start all over again.

I find it hard to stand back from the flow of my life and see God's overall direction. I tend to resist the times when I feel like I'm being splashed apart and thrown high into the unfamiliar, or when I'm sent to a quiet pool for rest when I'd rather be doing something active. But watching the river's steady journey, I know again that I, too, need to let myself be led by God, who can see beyond the little stretch of the journey that's visible to me.

MARCH 5   **Read Psalm 23**

Let God's promises flow from the verses into your heart. List those things for which you will not want or lack because of God's gifts to you. Offer those needs to God with an invitation to be the only Leader in your life this week.

MARCH 6   **Read Exodus 15:11-18**

You have been redeemed! God has already promised to lead you with unfailing love. Try, for one day, to follow with unfailing love. What are your expectations, as you begin, for how that will make a difference in your plans?

MARCH 7   **Read Jeremiah 31:7-9**

What is the pain in your life through which God wants to walk with you, to lead you on a path where you will not stumble? Look through your tears to the One who walks beside you. You are never alone.

MARCH 8   Read Deuteronomy 3:21-29

What "river" do you want to cross to which God seems to be saying, "No"? Write your feelings about that. How do you imagine God would respond? Write that, too. Continue this dialogue in your journal until it seems to be finished.

MARCH 9   Read Psalm 105

God's faithful leadership is seen in the recounting of Israel's history. Make a list of 10 to 12 events in your personal history when you have known God's leadership. Close your time with God, by reading verses 1 through 6 again as your personal prayer, from you to God.

MARCH 10   Read Matthew 4:18-22

This same Jesus continues to offer leadership on a daily basis. Take a few moments in silence and hear Jesus say to you, "Come, follow me." Where will that take you today?

MARCH 11   Read John 10:22-30

Grasp the meaning of this great promise for your life—that no one can take you away from God, your Leader. Rejoice in the joy of following!

Nurturer

As we rode our bicycles across the Mohave Desert in California, John and I stopped often to drink and douse our bodies with the coldest water we could find. We knew we couldn't last in that kind of heat for very long without water. The challenge, however, of living and traveling through those extremes, drew us with its desert charm.

Few houses were scattered across the parched plains, but the people who did live there shared enough water to provide us with periodic relief from the scorching sun. We were learning that the desert is no place to treat nature's seriousness lightly.

Almost forgetting what the color green looked like, we were excited one day to see a mound of lush foliage on the horizon. When we finally arrived in the small town, it didn't take long to figure out why that particular spot had been chosen for settlement.

A wide river flowed through the middle, flanked on both sides by the biggest, greenest trees we had seen in three days! After the near dehydration we had just experienced, we understood why both people and trees would choose to grow so close to the nourishment of water.

It makes sense, as well, that I would choose to grow close to the nurturing presence of God where I can be fed and watered. But so often, it seems, I willfully make plans to travel away from God. I believe, subconsciously, that I can do it on my own.

God, have mercy.

Lord, have mercy.

MARCH 12   Read Psalm 1

Plant yourself firmly in the rich soil of God's nurturing and loving law. Live verses 2, 3, and 6, and 1, 4, and 5 won't apply!

MARCH 13   Read John 7:38-44

We are fortunate enough to live after the resurrection, by which we know Jesus is the Christ. We still need to renew our faith each day, however, to enable the living water of His Spirit to flow through us. Is there a new part of your life through which you would like to invite Christ's Spirit to run today?

MARCH 14   Read Ezekiel 47:1-12

Our God has always nurtured the earth and its creatures into full potential. Where can you see God's blessing of abundance in your life? Write a prayer of praise and thanksgiving.

MARCH 15   Read Isaiah 30:23-25

God continually waits and wants to nurture the seeds you sow. Think of an act of love you can perform for someone today that will be like a refreshing river running through that person's life. Believe that God blesses your gift.

MARCH 16   Read Acts 16:13-15

Imagine that you are Lydia, going to the river expecting to find a place of prayer. (If possible, go sit by a river or meditate on a picture of a river.)

Let the Lord open your heart there, and come to you. Sit quietly, enjoying God's presence. Let the river drown out all but God's words to you.

MARCH 17   Read Jeremiah 17:7, 8

Who are the people who surround your roots, who nurture your life? Make a list of them. Choose one person to whom you will write a note, thanking him or her for helping to keep your "leaves green and bearing fruit."

MARCH 18   Read Revelation 22:1-5

In the last chapter of the Bible, we again receive the promise of the first Psalm—that God provides all we need. What are your needs today? God is waiting, wanting to give you the help you need.

Faithful

I almost lost faith in God one day.

I had planned a very special party to which I had invited many good friends. For weeks previous to this big event I prayed for good weather because it would be so much better if we could be outside. The plans were all set.

But on that day, I awoke to the sound of rain on the windows. Farmers in the area were undoubtedly waking with words of thanksgiving and praise to their faithful God who answered their prayers. But all God heard from me were accusations of not caring about me or my party.

Of course, beyond the emotion of the moment, I realize that my faith in God cannot depend on having my wishes fulfilled. Nor can God's faithfulness be defined by my random mood and the way I choose to interpret whatever situation I'm in.

It's fairly easy to understand that the weather is not a good measure of God's faithfulness. The principle of that prayer, however, comes alive in many other situations as well. I have faith in God to direct me in a job, a place to be, or how to live. When I can't hear the guidance within my timing, I begin to question God's caring, and work at my own answers.

This faith stuff is no easy matter! Maybe that's why we often talk about the leap of faith. I don't know where I'll land! But I can grow in my knowledge of God as the Faithful One as I put myself in positions of being able to see the world through God's eyes.

MARCH 19   Read Psalm 33

Make a list of the adjectives that describe who God is to you. Do
you see God as faithful, as One who merits your faith? It's a big
step. Why are you taking it. . . or not taking it?

MARCH 20   Read Jeremiah 2:18, 19

Look at your life from God's point of view. From where are you
drawing the water that energizes you? Write a letter to yourself from
God. Start it, "Dear (insert your name)," and sign it, "Love, God."

MARCH 21   Read Matthew 17:14-21

Note the correlation between the amount of faith one has and the
change it creates. Is it backwards? In whose eyes? Ask God
where you are being called to take a step of faith, to believe in
the impossible.

MARCH 22   Read Psalm 117

Read it again slowly. If a word or phrase strikes you as having
special meaning, stop and repeat it over and over until it becomes
a part of your breathing. Pray, not to finish, but just to be with
God for a time, like you do with your other friends. Begin and
end your time with God, as the Psalm does, in praise.

MARCH 23   Read Isaiah 42:1-9

This passage was written just for you—the chosen one in whom God delights! Whatever you are called to be or do, God promises to take hold of your hand. Relax as you spend time in the promise of God's faithfulness.

MARCH 24   Read Ephesians 3:14-21

You don't have to live by your power alone. Is Paul's prayer for the Ephesians also becoming fulfilled in you? Pray these verses for yourself. Then pray it for another person the Lord brings to your mind, maybe someone you are having a hard time loving.

MARCH 25   Read Amos 5:24

Where have the waters of your life flowed this past week, bringing justice and right-living to yourself, the friends around you, the world? Pray that your life may be a never failing stream of justice.

GOD
of the
Lakes

Comforter

A s I approached the edge of the lake, I felt a strange sensation of sadness welling up into my throat. Tears began to seep from behind my eyes. It was a familiar feeling, but not a recent one, and certainly not one I was expecting when I began this walk.

I was staying near the lake for the night and had come out to spend some time with God as the sun was setting. It had been a good day of traveling, and I couldn't figure out what I was grieving.

I remembered feeling a similar inner ache during high school, right after my boyfriend and I decided to go in different directions. It was also like the ache I felt as a child when I learned my dog had been killed on the road. But what was it tonight?

As I sat quietly by the edge of the lake, watching the ripples drift gently across with the evening breeze, I began to realize a sense of loneliness, stuck way down in the bottom of my stomach. I was remembering the last move I had made, away from people, a place, and a job that I loved.

I had missed them deeply at first, but as new people became my friends and as I got busy with my new job, I thought less and less about what I had left behind. Tonight, however, when I finally quieted myself, I could hear God saying, "There's another layer of loneliness I want to hear within you."

And the lake before me seemed to chime in with, "Go ahead. Let yourself feel the hurt on the banks of my calmness. God is already here to be your Comforter."

MARCH 26   Read Psalm 30

Commit a block of time to be silent—alone with God. Then read the Psalm as if you had written it, stopping to meditate on a line that draws your attention. Where are you needing God's comfort?

MARCH 27   Read Isaiah 40:1-5

Sometimes it seems hard to make time to spend alone with God, especially in those desert days when God seems to be far away, That's exactly the time, however, that Isaiah tells us to prepare the way for the Lord. That's exactly when God wants to come to us in tenderness, to comfort us. Rest in the comfort of God's tenderness for a while before going on to the many things awaiting you.

MARCH 28   Read Mark 6:45-52

Hear Jesus' words to you today, "Don't be afraid." To what is He referring? Talk to Jesus about your fear, knowing you don't have to face it alone. You may feel, at times, that Jesus is sending you on ahead, but He is right there, walking beside you.

MARCH 29   Read Matthew 14:25-36

Did you fall yesterday, like Peter, right after you decided to let Jesus take your fear? That happens to all of us at times. Like

Peter, too, let Jesus help you back up so you can keep learning to keep being used by God. What new step of faith is God taking with you today?

MARCH 30   **Read Psalm 119:49-56**

Does your suffering seem unfair or confusing? To take a step beyond frustration ask God to show you where Jesus felt the same kind of thing. What did He do with it? Let the knowledge of His understanding be your comfort.

MARCH 31   **Read Isaiah 52:8-12**

God MARCHes into your life today, offering comfort and joy. Keep your eyes open to seeing the Lord in everything you do and in everyone you meet.

APRIL 1   **Read John 14:25-27**

What a precious benediction for the week. Write Jesus a letter of acceptance for His loving provision of comfort.

Shepherd

When my parents went on a trip to Europe years ago, they not only returned with a gift for each of us children, but they also brought a bell for each of our sheep. They had been intrigued by the tinkling sounds coming from the pastures of Switzerland and determined that our flock of sheep would also wear bells around their necks. Ever after that, we knew exactly where our sheep were grazing.

Each evening the soft jingle of bells became a loud joyful clamor as the flock came running to the barn when they saw my brother appear. He was their caretaker and they knew they were about to get some special attention. He was the one who fed and watered them. He pulled them out of the squares in the wire fences where they repeatedly got their heads stuck while looking for greener grass on the other side. Using a bottle, he fed the lambs that otherwise would not have lived.

Our sheep knew my brother and knew that he would take care of them. They ran in from the fields every time he entered the barnyard. The sound of the bells seemed a fitting symbol for the joy they must have felt at his faithful return each day.

I wonder how my praise and gratefulness for the Great Shepherd's presence and care for me is heard in the world. If I really believe that the Lord is God, how will I respond? If I claim God as my Shepherd, I must, like the sheep, follow in total trust. I must respond in complete dependence. Sheep, by their very nature, cannot help but love the one who loves them. Oh, that I would become more sheep-like!

APRIL 2   Read Psalm 100

Read verse 3 over and over again until it becomes your own prayer. What shape will verses 1, 2, and 4 take in your life as you seek to respond to God's shepherding? Think of one way you will serve the Lord with gladness today. Let the bells ring!

APRIL 3   Read John 10:1-18

Spend time in silence and imagine that you hear Jesus calling you by name. Let yourself enjoy this overture of love. Let yourself believe that God is the Good Shepherd—not a hired hand!

APRIL 4   Read Mark 1:16-20

Jesus does call you by name. Imagine yourself in Simon's place. What do you need to leave behind to follow Jesus more closely?

APRIL 5   Read Luke 5:1-11

Yesterday we watched Simon leave his career to follow Jesus. Today, Jesus makes him more successful than ever in the career he just gave up! Can you let yourself believe that Jesus does not take anything away without giving you something better? Ask God for openness to see beyond the "boat" you're now in and your own ideas of what you need.

APRIL 6   Read Hebrews 13:20, 21

Put your own name into these verses along with those to whom
Paul is writing. What might be the "everything good" with which
the great Shepherd wants to equip you? List your ideas.

APRIL 7   Read Matthew 18:10-14

Close your eyes and imagine yourself shrinking in size and
significance until you are the tiniest "nobody" possible. Then
imagine Jesus coming to you, lifting you up, holding you, and
saying, "I love you." Let yourself bask in the knowledge of this
truth and in the presence of God. Feel yourself growing back to
size, clothed inside and out in God's gift of love.

APRIL 8   Read Mark 4:1-20

What kind of seed are you? In what kind of soil? Let the great
and trusted Shepherd, whom you've learned to know better in the
past few days, show you where you are to be planted today and
how to live in the soil in which you find yourself.

Ruler

*H*aving recently moved to Michigan, I'm having a lot of fun discovering its many lakes. Even though Minnesota is known as the land of 10,000 lakes, I'm finding out that Michigan has many to boast of as well. In our county alone there are 55 lakes.

The lakes here are thought to have been formed by the glaciers that came surging through this land years ago, sometimes depositing huge rocks and at other times gouging out holes of all sizes. Thus, lakes appear all over, even though there aren't springs to feed them. When it rains in excess, new lakes appear, and when there's a drought, some small ones disappear.

I am noticing the many stages that a lake goes through, from being a good-sized clear lake, like the one two miles from our home, to becoming so thick with vegetation that water can barely be seen, like the one behind our house that we call the marsh. Eventually, I'm told, they fill in with vegetation completely and the ground is solid again.

I am intrigued that God didn't just create the world long ago, put the lakes at their certain spots, and leave them there forever and ever. As it is, I feel like I can watch God in the act of creation again, every time I see another lake!

God was not only the world's first ruler, but continues to be our Living Ruler. Let the lakes witness to God's reign!

APRIL 9   Read Psalm 67

Read today's newspaper or think about the last newscast you watched or listened to. How do you see God at work in the world? God is the ruler of history and continues to rule. Look and listen to see where God's ways are being made known on earth. Make a list of the places, people, and events in which you've seen God's rule evident in the last 24 hours.

APRIL 10   Read Micah 5:1-5

The prophecy has been fulfilled! The promised ruler from Bethlehem has come, and we are to be those who can live securely in Jesus' greatness and peace. How does the peace Christ has brought to you compare to the world situation? Pray today for those who live amid conflict, that they will know the inner peace of the One who came to be our peace.

APRIL 11   Read Luke 1:26-38

God came to the world to be our ruler, but first had to have the consent of a human being. Put yourself in this story as Mary and imagine an angel of God appearing to you, announcing an impossible sounding task for you to do. How would you respond? How do you respond? What is God asking to do through your life?

APRIL 12   Read Luke 8:26-39

What would you have to report if Jesus said to you, "Go and tell how much God has done for you"? Imagine yourself sitting by the Sea of Galilee. What part of you would Jesus order to disappear to help make you a better person?

APRIL 13   Read Revelation 11:15-17

Find something that symbolizes God for you—a picture, a lake, a candle, a tree—whatever reminds you of God's presence with you as you pray. Imagine God's power and love flowing out from the space you're in now, engulfing your whole community, reaching out to your entire nation and then to the world. What can you do today to make God's kingdom more pervasive than it was yesterday?

APRIL 14   Read Isaiah 52:7

Spend time with God today, meditating on the stars or the clouds. First look up at them. Then imagine being one of them and looking down on the earth. What kind of message could you give the earth from that vantage point? If words cannot express your feelings, praise your Ruler with your silence.

APRIL 15   **Read I Chronicles 29:10-13**

Ask God's forgiveness for the times you have let yourself or others rule your life this week, rather than God. Then begin anew by reading David's prayer as your own.

GOD
of the
Rain

Refreshing

I sat in the warmth and security of my room, watching the rain falling softly on the street below. Umbrellas and hooded raincoats hurried past, hiding their inhabitants in protective custody.

Every once in a while, however, some strange souls strolled by, dressed in normal clothes and acting like the rain didn't exist. Maybe they liked getting wet!

I remembered walking in the rain with a friend one time who said, "Don't hurry. Let's just enjoy the rain and let it refresh us!"

That required beating back my natural impulses. I want the rain, of course, but only if I can watch the grass and crops soaking it up from my dry spot indoors! My main involvement with the rain is figuring out how to stay out of it.

How often I do the same in my relationship with God. I pray for God's presence to come alive in this world, but mostly, if I'm honest, I'm praying it for other people. I find it safer to watch God move in others' lives as I hide behind the security of my umbrella, than to let myself be soaked with God's presence. It is easier for me to pray that God will change my friends, than it is for me to be open to God changing my life.

For me it takes of lot of courage to pray not only for God's Spirit to be poured out on the world, but to also seek to be "soaked" myself by God's Refreshing Presence. As I watch the earth eagerly soak up the spring rain my desire grows.

APRIL 16 Read Psalm 65

As you begin another day, put aside your prayer requests and make a list of your past requests that have already been answered. Think of them as being showered upon you like a warm spring rain. Let your heart be soaked with thanksgiving.

APRIL 17 Read Proverbs 25:25

Close your eyes and imagine yourself working outside on an extremely hot day, dripping with sweat. Imagine, then, a person coming to you and handing you a cold drink. Who is it? Enjoy the refreshment of liquid as well as the refreshment of friendship.

APRIL 18 Read Song of Solomon 2:10-13

What music would a musician put to the rhapsody of this song? Play it in the background or in your mind as you imagine yourself the beloved who is called by God to blossom and flourish today.

APRIL 19 Read Psalm 72

Pray for the leaders of your community, and then of your country, that they may be as refreshing to those they lead as the rain is to the earth. Pray verse 16 for the people of another country that God brings to your mind.

APRIL 20   Read Hebrews 6:7, 8

Imagine yourself to be the ground, receiving the refreshing blessings of God's love again today. What fruit of the Spirit is leafing out from you in return? Think of a way to share this "fruit" with a family member.

APRIL 21   Read Colossians 2:6-15

What trespasses come to your mind as you read verses 13 and 14? If there is one that continues to haunt you, write it on a piece of paper, imagine God's forgiveness raining on it, and watch the ink become blurred beyond recognition. Throw it away and forget it as Christ has.

APRIL 22   Read Philemon 4-7

It's another of Paul's beautiful salutations! Think of someone you could add to Paul's greetings because of the love and faith she has, or the joy and encouragement you receive from him. Thank God for this personal example of Christ to you.

Cleansing Power

I'll never forget the first garden I had of my very own. Having moved from the country, where our family had shared the work and pleasure of a big garden, to a city with only enough dirt to grow tomatoes in the flower beds, I thought gardening in that setting was simply impractical. So I was thrilled when a friend offered me the use of a large patch of ground behind her house.

Soon after our conversation, I visited my new garden space on a morning following a hard rain, and I saw what likely explained my generous loan. The plot of ground, which already held my dreams of a bountiful vegetable harvest, was covered with rocks! The rain had washed away what I thought were clumps of dirt to reveal what was really there.

I was disappointed, but I was also glad for the more realistic view the rain had provided. Clearing rocks, thereafter, became a continuing part of my garden project. It took extra work, but nothing could have grown if I had left the rocks there.

I believe that God's cleansing power comes to me in the same way the rain came to my garden. As long as I don't look beneath the surface, I can feel like I don't need much work on who I am. When I allow God to wash the "top dirt" away, however, my sinfulness is revealed, and I can see more clearly the things that are preventing my growth.

Sin in my life doesn't disappear with any more magic than the rocks in my garden. God does provide the cleansing power, however, to not only show me who I really am, but to also help me continue to grow. It is a cleansing I cannot duplicate or earn. All I can do is accept it and do my part in the cultivation.

APRIL 23   Read Psalm 118

This is a song for Palm Sunday. Insert your family name in the litany of verse 3 and imagine your family joining the triumphal procession of Jesus into your neighborhood. Live today in the certainty of Jesus' presence within and about you.

APRIL 24   Read Numbers 19

What ceremonial-type cleansing do you find yourself doing? Chastising yourself? Blaming yourself repeatedly? Accepting the blame of others? Remember again from yesterday, Jesus' triumphal entry, the purpose of which was to abolish the need for ceremonial cleansing forever. Thank God that you are no longer bound by such laws as you read about in today's Scripture.

APRIL 25   Read Ezekiel 36:22-32

Receive verses 25-29 as a light, warm, shower, a personal gift God sprinkles on you today. Through this act of cleansing and compassion, God's holiness is revealed in you. Relax for a few minutes, soaking in the awesomeness of this truth.

APRIL 26   Read Hebrews 10:19-39

Faith is an unearned gift to be received, just as the earth receives the unearned rains. Wash your face with warm water, letting it symbolize the cleansing Jesus' love and gift of faith provide you in a fresh way today.

APRIL 27   Read Hosea 10:12

Let your seeking of the Lord be done in waiting. Sit quietly, letting God come to you. What is the gift God has to rain on you today?

APRIL 28   Read Ephesians 5:21-33

Who in your life helps you feel more clean and more whole by the way they love and give themselves to you? Be good to yourself today, and make plans to spend time with that person soon!

APRIL 29   Read Isaiah 44:21-23

Replace "Jacob" and "Israel" with your name and receive this as a letter to you from God for the cleansing power that has been at work in you this week, perhaps in a new way.

Almighty

*T*his morning I awoke to the gentle sound of rain outside my window and the smell of spring air drifting into the room. Actually I awoke several times. "Oh, that sounds so peaceful," I thought. "I'll just listen to it for a few minutes before I get up," and I was lulled right back to sleep. Other mornings I've awakened to the sound of a thunderous rain which sounds like I'm being given a direct order to get up and get moving!

When I was little I thought that thunder was the voice of God and I often wondered what God was saying. I still believe that God speaks to us in the thunder and in the gentleness of this morning's rain, as well as in the moisture which quietly vaporizes from the earth on other mornings.

Scientists know more today about what causes the sound of thunder, and meteorologists can predict rain more accurately than those who lived in Old Testament times. God is the One who created the world to work with such intricate order and predictability. I find that more incredible than a God who would choose the weather at random each day!

Each morning when I awake, whether it's raining or not, I see God reigning in the world by the fact that order exists. The more I learn about the laws of nature, the more they demand my respect. We are able to predict the rain and watch its movements—one more testimony to God's ultimate control, as certain now as in the days of Elijah. God the Almighty reigns!

APRIL 30   **Read Psalm 84**

Underline or jot down the phrases in this Psalm that suggest a
picture in your mind of what the Lord's dwelling place looks like.
Draw, color, or paint your favorite room, and place yourself
inside.

MAY 1   **Read I Kings 17:1-16**

How does the picture of Elijah's new dwelling place by the Wadi
Cherith compare to yesterday's picture of your favorite room in
the Lord's dwelling place? Can you imagine the Almighty God
present in both pictures? Journal about the room in which you
find yourself. Is it lush or barely furnished? Know that God's
presence is in both places.

MAY 2   **Read I King 17:7**

Imagine Elijah's dismay as the Wadi, with which God has provided
him, dries up. Write a letter of encouragement and hope to him,
reminding him that God remains Almighty even though it may
not always feel like it. Then read the rest of chapter 17, imagining
that you are with him.

MAY 3   **Read I Kings 18:1-40**

Sit back and give yourself time to become immersed in this familiar story. As the drama unfolds, watch the Almighty hero, for whom Elijah works, stay in control. Give your control of the day ahead to this same Almighty God.

MAY 4   **Read I Kings 18:41-46**

After three years, God sent rain. Whom do you know who seems to be living in a drought of not experiencing the rain of God? Find a way to be the hands and feet of the Almighty to that person as a reminder of God's love.

MAY 5   **Read Revelation 19:6, 7**

Look at a map of the world. Let your prayer be for all the people of the earth, so that this day will see us drawing closer together in the thunderous chorus of these verses.

MAY 6   **Read Judges 6:36-40**

As you watch Gideon's hesitancy to believe, watch also the patience of God who can do anything alone, but chooses to wait for Gideon. Thank the Almighty that you are cradled in these same patient hands.

Sovereign

I have recently received encouragement from *An Interrupted Life*, from the diaries of Etty Hillesum. Etty was a Jewish woman living in Amsterdam during Hitler's reign of terror, which eventually claimed her life. In this setting, she writes about her everyday life, about the inner workings of her soul.

Etty's honesty in describing the ups and downs of her emotions is refreshing and inspiring—maybe because I have often discounted those incongruities within myself, hiding behind the illusion that life should always be good. I can praise the sovereignty of the Lord as long as my life is exciting and generous. I immediately question God about difficulties, however, and wonder if God is even around.

As a human being, capable of a large variety of emotions, I rejoice in a God who accepts me in each of them. Rain, and its many moods, reflects both my own range of feelings, as well as God's ability to be quietly—or powerfully—present. Rain, in it's variety of forms, is like the many ways God comes.

Rain is sometimes barely noticeable, a light misting. In this form it can be either a pleasant variation in the weather or a nuisance, depending on how I receive it. A heavy rain makes the farmers happy, but it can also negatively interrupt the lives of others, especially if it comes in the middle of their picnic! Heavy continuous rains can create the worst disaster of a lifetime. People die, homes are ruined, and fields wash away in floods.

Note the ways in which the rain has come to you this spring. Let that remind you of your Sovereign God, who comes to you with variety. Let the rain be an occasion for you to take a break from your normal routine and listen to your soul.

MAY 7   **Read Psalm 135**

How has God's sovereignty been displayed in your life so far this year? After verse 12 list the signs and wonders you have experienced. Close your time of prayer with verse 21, changing "Jerusalem" to your home place.

MAY 8   **Read Isaiah 45:1-8**

Close your eyes and imagine you are God, watching you. Ask to be shown what God would like to be and do and think through you. When you are ready, go back to being yourself and give God your response. Reread verse 8.

MAY 9   **Read James 5:13-20**

Think of a modern-day person whom you think of as a spiritual giant, in the same way James remembered Elijah. Can you believe that the sovereign God wants to work through your prayer of faith just as powerfully? Let the truth of this knowledge fall on you like a gentle rain.

MAY 10   Read Ezekiel 34:25-31

Make a list of the blessings God has showered upon you in the
past few days. Let your attitude of thankfulness carry you into
the day's challenges.

MAY 11   Read Psalm 47

Sing, play, or write a song of praise in honor of God's sovereign
rule in your life again today.

MAY 12   Read Isaiah 50:4-10

Close your eyes and imagine listening to the rain. Then smell it,
taste it, watch it, feel it on your skin. Let the rain, and the use of
all of your senses, remind you of the One who is above all and in
all.

MAY 13   Read Acts 4:23-30

Go for a five- or ten-minute walk, looking for signs of God's
sovereignty. Imagine God's one hand on your shoulder and the
other pointing out what you might notice.

Perfect

I know a man who tells of a night when, in an act of powerful revelation, God sent rain on the car he was driving, while the cars and buildings all around him remained dry. This experience followed a period of his crying out for a sign of God's existence. While God chose that form of miracle for one who needed to see it, I am more often aware of the truth in Matthew 5:45, "[God] sends rain on the righteous and the unrighteous." Usually when it rains, the gardens that need it for growth get it, as well as the backyard where we had been hoping to have a picnic!

Somehow, I find it easier to accept the chancy way in which rain falls on me and my plans, than the randomness with which other things in life land on me. When life is full of good things, I'm thankful or, shamefully, take it for granted that life should be good.

When life is difficult and painful, however, or when I see the ugliness within myself, I cry out to my "unjust" God in anguish. A hard life seems wrong, and the perfection to which my perfect God calls me seems impossible to attain.

But if I think I am close to the perfection I see in Jesus Christ, it may be time to get down on my hands and knees and beg forgiveness. That was Adam's and Eve's sin—wanting to be perfectly God.

My calling to perfection, rather, must be a call to perfect humanity. It is a call to know myself, sins and all, and to accept God's perfect healing love.

MAY 14   Read Psalm 18:30-50

Can you believe that having anger, and then admitting it to God, is not wrong, but perfectly human? God knows about it anyway, so you may as well let it into your prayers. Write your prayer of anger about the injustice of which you are most aware today. Let the Perfect One receive it so that you may begin to let go of it.

MAY 15   Read Matthew 5:43-48

Does it feel like your world is raining on you today, or like the sun is shining? Let yourself be wherever you are, without thinking you need to move on quickly. Accept this, not as a sign of your evil or goodness, but as a sign of your humanity. Praise God who is over all in perfection.

MAY 16   Read Deuteronomy 32:1-4

What "song" would you, like Moses, like to rain down upon the earth? Write a few lines of praise in your journal. Then color raindrops on top of it as a symbol of how your life has been nourished by the perfect work of the Lord.

MAY 17   **Read Psalm 119:89-96**

Like an Olympian knows, to strive toward human perfection is to narrow one's focus of energy. God's perfection, however, is boundless and exceedingly broad. Is your present life centered more on your own narrow perfection or on enjoying God's boundless perfection? Are you happy with this focus? If not, decide on one "attitude adjustment" you can make today.

MAY 18   **Read Matthew 19:16-26**

What is it that keeps you from serving God above all else? A possession? A friend? The use of your time? What change is Jesus asking for in your life? Think of returning this part of yourself to God—not to disappear, but to be transformed.

MAY 19   **Read Colossians 3:12-14**

Do these verses sound like an impossible task? They are—alone. Close your eyes and meditate on the fact that you are one of God's chosen people, holy and loved.

MAY 20   **Read Hebrews 12:1-13**

For what have you felt disciplined by God? Write a letter to God, expressing how you felt or feel about it, and listen for God's response. Can you believe the promise of verse 6?

Foundation

A room was once added on to the original brick structure of the house in which we currently live. It's a small house, and the former residents were likely grateful for the extra space this little lean-to provided. Over the years, however, the poorly built structure has taken a lot of wear and tear. Rains have left their mark. The boards around the bottom are rotting out, the roof leaks and the framework which joins the room to the brick wall of the house has pulled away so that wind and rain come in freely. If we want to use that room, our only option is to tear it down and rebuild it with new material. Fortunately, the foundation was laid well and is the one part we would not have to redo.

The room reminds me daily of the Scriptures which refer to God as the Rock or Foundation upon which I need to build my life. It is a given, when physically building a house or when metaphorically building my life, that time, energy, and materials are wasted unless they are used to first pour a good foundation.

A building, or my life, however, won't last long if I am not also careful about how I build onto that good foundation. Part of what

God offers is the gift of the best foundation. Accepting that is where I need to begin. How I build on it, then, is the work for which I need to continue to rely on God's strength.

MAY 21   **Read Psalm 144**

What blessings are falling on you today? Make a list of them in thanksgiving to the One who gives them to you. Think of them as a foundation on which to build your day.

MAY 22   **Read Matthew 7:24-27**

Write down the activities you have planned for today. Separate the ones you know are God-inspired from the ones on which you haven't yet consulted God. Ask for wisdom to hear the words and leading of God before you get busy!

MAY 23   **Read Isaiah 26:1-9**

Imagine sitting on a huge comfortable rock in the middle of a stream. While there, read again verse 4 and think of God as the Rock you can trust for your foundation. Rest here as long as the rock is comfortable.

MAY 24   **Read Ephesians 2:19-22**

Who are the others who join you as members of God's household?
Draw a "prayer wall," inserting the names of these people on
each brick. Choose one or two that you will remember to pray
for throughout the day in a special way.

MAY 25   **Read I Corinthians 3:10-17**

Write a note to one of the people whose name appeared on your
wall yesterday. Thank that person for helping to uphold you.

MAY 26   **Read I Timothy 6:17-19**

Do you think of yourself as rich? To whom are you comparing
yourself? Now compare yourself to someone on the other end
of the economic scale to get a different perspective on your
wealth. Think of something you can give away that will make you
more equal with one who is not as rich as you are. Do it!

MAY 27   **Read Hebrews 11:1-16**

Remember the foundation Christ has laid for your life. What does
your faith suggest will be remembered about you after you die?
Write your epitaph, in faith.

GOD
of the
Raging
Waters

Judge

Titus was one of the most gentle men I ever knew. I admired his compassion for every person he met. How, I wondered, did he find the energy and time to care for so many? I respected his efforts to seek out people of different races and cultures so he could learn more about them. I was grateful to be one of his "students," benefiting from his contagious love and acceptance of people. He reminded me many times of Jesus.

One day I was with Titus when he became enraged. He watched a poor woman, with no power to defend herself, being treated unfairly. He stepped in, forcefully speaking up for the woman in angry words until the attacker backed down in apologies.

The poor woman was grateful. I was dumbfounded! Could this be the same Titus? What had happened to the gentle man, full of Christ's love?

When he returned to our group, minutes later, Titus was his familiar gentle self. As we talked about what had happened, I saw that he was not angry at the man, only at what he had done to the woman. He had not stepped, in this act, outside of his role of being a follower of Jesus. He was emulating Jesus, who cleansed the temple in anger over the injustices being performed there by the rich and powerful, against the poor and powerless. He was like Jesus who stood by the woman caught in adultery.

I was shown, that day, a broader view of God—One who incorporates acceptance and judgment in the same being, One in whom anger does not dispel love, One who does not have a weak backbone, but rules the entire world with a gentle strength.

MAY 28   Read Psalm 50:1-6

Is it a scary thought for you, or a comforting one, that God is Judge? Write a letter to God expressing your feelings. Write, too, God's reply to you.

MAY 29   Read Job 40:6-14

Contrast your reaction to a normal summer thunderstorm as a child with your response now. Has your broadened understanding of what causes them helped to diminish your fears? How have you seen or experienced God as Judge in ways that help your fears diminish and your respect for God grow?

MAY 30   Read Genesis 6

At this point in your life, would you be included in the family of Noah who does all that God commands you? Are there parts of your life God would like to "flood out"? Write a prayer of confession and let God assure you of pardon.

MAY 31   Read Matthew 24:36-51

As a child of God, you do not need to fear being swept away in surprise, as happened in the days of Noah. Live today as if it were to be your last. Do your plans need to change?

JUNE 1   Read II Peter 2

If people come to your mind, as you read this passage, whom you perceive to be false prophets, pray for each one. Picture yourself on the witness stand as you get a chance to speak, reserving the judge's chambers for God.

JUNE 2   Read Jude 1-16

Jude paints a graphic picture of a stormy, broken world. Think of similar scenes in your own world, and, for each scene, picture God in the midst of the storm. What do your pictures include?

JUNE 3   Read Psalm 75

Pray with the aid of a globe or world map, imagining all the earth's many inhabitants. Thank God for being the pillar that keeps the earth whole, despite its damage.

Shelter

My three-year-old daughter, Maria, believes that rain falls for her personal enjoyment! When I'm in the mood, I can share her enthusiasm! I won't melt in the rain. It can stimulate my senses if I let it, as I see, feel, taste, smell, and hear the rain splashing on me, drop by drop, until I'm completely soaked and dripping. Puddles can chase away the boredom and heat of summer. So occasionally I join her as the rain begins, helping to hunt the biggest puddles.

But even Maria runs for shelter and a towel when the rain turns into a downpour. And no matter how much we have tried to instill within her a fascination for thunder and lightning, she dives under cover when a storm comes by! Her "brave" dog tries to do the same. It seems instinctual for animals to hide when the water that refreshes suddenly appears out of control.

Fortunately, the God of the gentle snow, nourishing springs, bubbling brooks, peaceful lakes, and refreshing rain, also becomes a shelter when waters begin to rage. With the exception of destroying the whole earth by a flood, God has not promised to keep us from other storms. And we often see and hear of damage done by raging waters, typhoons, tropical storms, and floods.

God has not promised to keep me immune from turmoil or fear or anguish. God does, however, offer to be a Shelter when the world within and around me is raging. I only need to recognize that that shelter is there and let myself relax in Its protection.

JUNE 4   **Read Psalm 55**

Draw a picture of God sheltering you. What is in the raging water from which you are finding protection? Let God hold you in the midst of the storm.

JUNE 5   **Read Genesis 7**

Imagine yourself in this story as one of Noah's grandchildren. Sit on Noah's lap as you listen to the endless rain, and let him tell you a story about what is happening. How does he describe God? How does he explain how your family was chosen to be protected?

JUNE 6   **Read Psalm 124**

List the "enemies" in your life: people, things, or circumstances that rage around you like a storm. Imagine the shelter of God lining your body so your inner soul can relax and find peace.

JUNE 7   **Read Isaiah 4:2-6**

Go for a walk and choose a sign you will see throughout your day. Let it be a sign to you of the shelter God will be to you, as the cloud and fire were to the survivors of Zion.

JUNE 8   Read Isaiah 54:9-17

Receive this eternal covenant of peace as a love letter to you from God. If there is a word or phrase that seems especially good to you, read it over and over, like you rehearsed the words of your first love.

JUNE 9   Read James 1:1-7

How can God be your Shelter and at the same time allow you to be tossed around in raging waters? If you can't put the two into the same God, talk to someone whom you think may understand.

JUNE 10   Read Job 10:1-9

Do you sometimes wonder, like Job, if you will be destroyed if you allow God to shape and mold you? What is God's answer to you? Write down the answer that comes to you and place it securely in your heart.

Calm

Murray came bursting into the Sunday morning worship service, drenched from his hat to his boots. He was gasping for breath and obviously in a daze as he repeatedly exclaimed, "I can't believe it. I CAN'T BELIEVE IT!"

In the front row sat the children who had been called together for a special story. They had been told that a friend of Jesus was coming to see them and they would be asked to decide who it was. They had no preparation, however, for what had just come through the door! They looked enthralled as this man, whom they knew as Tara's and Anna's father, hurriedly wiped his dripping face and tried to catch his breath. It didn't take long for even the youngest child to recognize impetuous Peter as he began to tell his story. It was the familiar story of Jesus asleep in a boat with his disciples as a fierce storm began to rage. "Peter" told of his terror in that storm, until he heard Jesus tell the storm to stop and watched Him take control. Then he said his intense fear turned to amazement and finally shame that he had so little faith.

Since that Sunday I've experienced this episode in other situations in my life. I have never been caught literally in a boat on a stormy lake, but I have often felt Peter's panic and fear, while I let Jesus stay calmly in the bottom of my boat!

I've sometimes wondered why the disciples were so terrified of that storm, when the miraculous Jesus, whom they knew so well, was right there with them. But why do I often let panic take over when the calmness Jesus embodies is right beside me too? The question becomes, how can I house God's calm within me?

JUNE 11   Read Psalm 107:23-32

Are you in the midst of a stormy time in your life, as in verses 26 and 27, or in the aftermath, as in verses 29 and 30, in which you can see how God calmed the waters? Write verse 31 on a card to accompany you throughout the day, as a reminder of your Lord who has the power to calm.

JUNE 12   Read Mark 4:35-41

Relax and quiet yourself for a few minutes, imagining yourself to be in the bottom of a boat until you can feel Jesus' words, "Peace! Be still!" seeping into your head and flowing to every muscle and bone of your body.

JUNE 13   Read Luke 8:22-25

How long were you able to meditate yesterday on Jesus commanding peace in your life? Try the same meditation today. Imagine Jesus rebuking the raging waters that stormed in to disturb your peace yesterday.

JUNE 14   Read Genesis 8

If God were to command a flood in your life to dispel all of the evil, what would be left as the waters recede? Celebrate the goodness God retains through you in a prayer of thanksgiving.

JUNE 15   Read Jonah 1

What is the sin that seems unforgivable to you? Who might God be calling, as Jonah was called to Nineveh, to declare God's forgiveness of this sin within you? Make yourself available to God's love through this person, and let yourself believe the good news.

JUNE 16   Read Habakkuk 3

Revive the four-year-old child deep within yourself and allow him or her to draw, paint, or color a picture of the sun warming the waters and the earth. Add yourself to the picture, and let yourself be warmed by God's calming love.

JUNE 17   Read Philippians 4:4-9

Think of someone your life will touch today, who could use God's peace. Let yourself be used as the transmitter of this peace by your words or action. Be aware of the peace with which God keeps you.

Miraculous

*T*hat's an easy one for me!" Mark spoke up immediately in response to the question, "When have you experienced, without a doubt, that God was at work in your life in an extraordinary way?" "I was only four or five years old, but I still remember the details clearly," Mark said.

He went on to tell about a day soon after his family moved from Los Angeles, California, to Amarillo, Texas. He didn't remember details of the move itself, but he vividly recalled that soon after settling into their new home, a Texas storm thundered in. Because of the dry air and the wide, open, flat country that stretches on and on in Texas, the thunder is extraordinarily loud, the lightning flashing through the sky can be seen for miles, and the raging wind and rain continue for hours.

Without even knowing about the threat of tornadoes in such storms, Mark still became hysterical with fright. Nothing could console him.

Finally, his mother suggested that they pray and ask Jesus to comfort him. As she prayed, Mark was overcome with complete peace and was soon asleep!

Memories of this tremendous power of God in nature, combined with the overwhelming sense of security Mark was given in the midst of it, has permanently shaped his view of God. He doesn't expect God to perform the same miracle every time he is frightened, but because of that early formative experience, Mark now lives in the knowledge and assurance of that capacity of God's. I am coming to believe that the God of miracles can be especially evident in the raging storms of my life, even more than in times of calm and peace.

JUNE 18 Read Psalm 106:1-12

The Psalmist calls you, too, to remember. Take a few minutes to remember an experience you have had like Mark (page 87) and like the Israelites walking to safety between the raging waters of the Red Sea, when you have known the miracle of God in some extraordinary way.

JUNE 19 Read Jonah 2

Have you ever felt like you were being drowned in a flood or swallowed alive? Write a prayer of thanksgiving for deliverance if it's a memory of the past, or a prayer of supplication if it's what you're feeling today.

JUNE 20 Read Numbers 20:1-11

If God commanded Moses to strike a rock to meet your needs today, what would flow from it? Let God know your needs and open yourself to the miraculous.

JUNE 21 Read John 2:1-11

Jesus at first seemed to rebuke his mother's suggestion. Perhaps this would not have been His first miracle, however, if she had not persisted. You, too, can feel invited to persist in letting Jesus know your needs. Maybe you will repeat yesterday's prayer. Maybe today holds a new request. Write it in your journal.

JUNE 22   **Read II Kings 2:1-22**

Think of a person or family who seem to be surrounded with raging waters of death or misery. How can you be the salt thrown in their water to help bring them closer to wholeness?

JUNE 23   **Read Exodus 7:14-24**

Think of a way God is working in the world to bring good out of what appears to be as awful as the Nile waters turned to blood. If you cannot see the good right now, let your prayer be to see the world through the eyes of God.

JUNE 24   **Read Isaiah 35**

Close your eyes and imagine all the changes of verses 5-10 happening all around you. Join the celebration of this new world order!

GOD
of Our
Tears

Provider

A s I drove up to the home where my brother, his wife, and their four children have made a life for themselves in the woods of Tennessee, I was once again impressed by how beautifully they live. The house at the end of the long, winding lane began ten years ago as a one-room dwelling. Ron built it himself. As the family grew, so did the house.

They added other comforts as they had money and energy available—electricity, a refrigerator, a bigger garden, and a well from which to draw water. They continue, however, to live without plumbing and to cook on a wood stove.

I love to visit them because there I see such a concrete display of God's goodness in providing for their needs from day to day. When I'm there, I live closer to God's creation. I watch the squirrels and rabbits on the way to the outhouse. Special plants and birds flourish in the woods that surround their house. When I help chop and carry firewood, I am part of the very direct way in which nature gives back to us.

When I am at their home, I feel connected to a larger world. It is a world in which God has provided for many people through the ages. On this same plot of ground one can see evidence of fires built by Native Americans on rocks that house a spring of water. I wonder how many people and animals have had their needs met here. We find arrowheads in the soil. I wonder how hard life was for those who have lived here. What did they cry about, laugh about?

JUNE 25   Read Psalm 107:33-43

Picture in your mind all the people and animals who have, at some time, lived on the piece of earth where you are now living. Picture their needs and how God has provided, including the ones you have today.

JUNE 26   Read Isaiah 43:19-21

What is the new thing God wants to do in you? Is it accompanied by resistance and tears or the joy of welcome? Ask God to provide the help you need to see what is springing forth.

JUNE 27   Read Luke 4:14-21

Celebrate the fact that there is no one for whom Jesus did not come. How can you join Jesus in providing for one need you see in the world today?

JUNE 28   Read Isaiah 61:1-3

How do these verses, written long before Jesus stood up in the temple to fulfill them, validate His Lordship in your life? In what ways are you, too, called to fulfill this scripture?

JUNE 29   Read Matthew 6:25-34

"Do not worry" sometimes seems like an impossible command. Go ahead and write a letter to Jesus concerning one of the things about which you are now worried. Let Him be your Provider in holding your fears, wiping away your tears, or crying with you.

JUNE 30   Read Isaiah 41:17-20

Where in the world today, as you see it in your community or hear it in the news, do you see God at work, fulfilling the promise of these verses? Let that recognition be your prayer.

JULY 1   Read II Corinthians 9:6-15

Repeat verse 15 until you can say it with your eyes closed. Let the words flow with the rise and fall of your breathing. Take it with you for a reminder throughout the day.

Home

We were on a weekend retreat. The theme for our time together was "Family," and the leader was taking us on an imaginary guided journey through our childhood. We began as far back as our memories allowed us to go, and saw again the house we lived in, the yard, the spot where we most often went to be alone, the dining room table, our bedroom, and so on.

As we came back to the whole group later, some spoke of this experience as a wonderful time of remembering joyful, peaceful, and fun times. Others sobbed, recalling moments of heartache and pain. Still others cried with grief for those who have since died. Most of us moved back and forth between happy and sad feelings as we traveled from place to place, triggering varied memories and "seeing" the people with whom we shared those early days.

We continued to talk throughout the weekend about our families, both those that are real and those that are still ideals, the ones we are continuing to form. And we were reminded of the humanness of our homes. It is a given, the speaker said, that we must each forgive our parents. None of them was perfect. No home is perfect.

It is helpful for me to think and talk about how my childhood home has shaped who I am. It is also helpful to consider the home I am currently part of shaping and to see God as my only true Home. God is the Parent for whom I long. God is the accepting Parent to whom I come Home with all my fears, joys, pain, and blah times. As an adult, Jesus had no house to go to for His Home. He showed me, however, in his relationship to God, the basic ingredients of a Home, the place where I am accepted and loved, whatever my changing moods and feelings. God, through Jesus, is my perfect Home.

JULY 2   Read Psalm 137:1-6

Join the children of Israel in a foreign land, as they remember their ideals of home in Jerusalem. Let yourself remember one of the unrealized dreams of your ideal home. Pray for God's healing of that memory.

JULY 3   Read Philippians 3:17-21

While God allows choices that sometimes cause "home" to carry painful memories, God also gives us citizenship in heaven—our perfect Home. Draw a symbol of your belonging in God's Home. Then place a symbol of your human home within it. How does this alter your view of your current situation?

JULY 4   Read Matthew 8:18-22

Consider Jesus' lifestyle of having no consistent place to lay his head. Then write a prayer of gratefulness for the blessing of your home.

JULY 5   Read Jeremiah 50:4, 5

What place does God have in your home? Could a stranger walk in and know that your household seeks the Lord? Look around you and be aware of how where you live shows evidence of your true Home.

JULY 6   Read II Corinthians 5:1-10

Be aware of someone in the news or someone whom you know, who has lost his or her home for some reason. Pray that God's reality and Christ as Home will be shown to that person, through yourself or another.

JULY 7   Read Ephesians 1:3-14

Close your eyes and imagine Jesus telling you the story of your adoption into His family. Listen as He describes His joy and dreams for your life. Let yourself rest in Jesus' love.

JULY 8   Read Colossians 3:15-17

Write a note of gratitude to one who has helped you feel at home in the body of Christ.

Healer

*I*n my part-time job, I work with pregnant women who are in recovery from an addiction to a substance of abuse, usually alcohol, cocaine, or both. While talking with a co-worker recently, I was reminded of one of the realities of life—it's not easy!

Our task with these women is not to tell them that life will be grand and glorious if they quit using their substance of choice. Rather, it is to help them face the difficulties that life will surely hold, but face them in some way other than by using the escape of a mood-altering chemical. No one can protect them from the pain that is sure to come, but we can offer to be with them in the midst of those difficulties, just as we know the healing God has brought in the middle of our own.

If we, as staff, try to teach only the joy and beauty Christ offers, we are treating these women as infants, encouraging them to seek only self-satisfaction. We are ignoring the difficulties of their lives that likely led them to seek their initial escape through drugs.

For any of us, addicted or not, to develop a relationship with God the Healer, we have to acknowledge what within us is in need of healing. To be able to laugh in the joy of Christ, we need to also recognize the freedom to cry with Christ. To get beyond an escapism mentality, we need to be willing to feel our own pain, to share in the pain of others, and to see tears as essential in the process of healing.

JULY 9   **Read Psalm 6**

Can you imagine how this Psalmist's prayer of tears can be used by God as part of the healing process? Remember the last time you cried. Was God with you in your tears? Pray that God will help you remember, the next time you cry, that healing is happening, even in the midst of your pain.

JULY 10   **Read Mark 8:22-26**

What would you like to see more clearly in your life? Close your eyes and imagine Jesus coming to you like He came to the blind man. Let Him help you focus on what is most important for you right now.

JULY 11   **Read John 5:1-9**

Whom do you know who is in so much misery that they don't realize Jesus is their Healer? Think of a way you can help lower them into the healing waters of Jesus' love today by a note, a call, a visit, or some other reminder that someone cares.

JULY 12   **Read Genesis 15:1-6**

Think about the difficulties in your life. Read this as your personal prayer for today. Replace Abram's name with your own and

receive God's promise to you as well:
"The word of the Lord came to (insert your name).
Do not be afraid, (insert your name),
I am your shield, your very great reward."
Pray this verse for others who come to your mind as well.

JULY 13   Read Exodus 15:22-27

Think of a time God has "sweetened the bitter water" you were drinking. Offer your Healer a prayer of retrospective thanksgiving.

JULY 14   Read II Kings 5:9-14

Humbling yourself before God can be difficult! It can also be what heals you. Search yourself to know if you, like Naaman, are being asked to give up some prideful element of defense. Alone before God, open yourself to the Healer's touch.

JULY 15   Read Matthew 26:69-75

Write a prayer of confession for the times you have refused to let Christ be recognized in your life—either by yourself or those who watch you. Then receive the Healer's forgiveness.

Redeemer

A bumper sticker on the car proclaimed loudly, "THERE IS POWER IN THE BLOOD!"

"What do you think of that?" Morrie asked his friend, pointing at the slogan. His buddy did not claim to know much about Christianity, and Morrie wondered how someone unfamiliar with what those words meant would react to them.

"It sounds pretty gory to me," replied his friend, dismissing it all. Morrie thought the smiley face on one end of the sticker and the glittering cross on the other probably didn't help much in showing the deep meaning that he knew the phrase held.

The pain and the powerless position of being on a cross makes me want to move quickly through that part of Jesus' life. I would rather contemplate the power Jesus came to possess because he went through that experience. It is simply more pleasant, more appealing, to share in the joy of the resurrection than the tears of the cross.

Yet without understanding Jesus to be my Redeemer, I lose much of who God is. When I paraphrase John 3:16 in my experience, I remember that. "God loves me so much that God sent Jesus to me, so that because of His life and death and life, I, too, can live forever." His life is not complete without the tears of his death.

Thankfully, that heartache is not the end, but I find it helpful to sometimes share more fully in Oneness with Christ by pausing to share the tears of the cross. This is the Jesus who understands my tears, my heartaches, and my pain and holds me in all of my confusion.

JULY 16   **Read Psalm 126**

Is this time of your life more one of sowing in tears or of reaping
with joy? Whichever it is, invite God to be with you in it, knowing
it will not last forever. Be willing, however, to live your current
situation as fully as possible today.

JULY 17   **Read Revelation 21:1-5**

This is what will last forever. What does God want to redeem in
your life already today, to continue the process of making all
things new?

JULY 18   **Read Psalm 102**

Close your eyes and think about the most painful part of your life
right now. Then imagine Jesus coming to you to redeem, or make
whole, that part of you. How does He come? What does He do?
Write a response in your journal.

JULY 19   **Read Luke 21:20-28**

Read the newspaper or listen to the news today, imagining Jesus,
who has already made redemption available to each person and
situation about which you hear, reading or listening with you.

JULY 20   Read Hebrews 10:11-18

Many of us get caught at times trying to earn the forgiveness Christ has already provided for us. Write an acceptance speech to your Redeemer for the gift.

JULY 21   Read Job 19:21-27

Through his tears, Job recognizes the living hope of his Redeemer who is with him in his pain and will also help him through it. Thank God that you have been given the same gift.

JULY 22   Read Isaiah 49:1-7

Maybe the painful parts of your experience are exactly the elements God can use to bring Christ's redemption to others. Think of one way your tears have enabled your servanthood and given you a sense of mission to others.

Forgiver

At three years of age, Maria seems to take great delight in frustrating me, her mother! Granted, she doesn't do it in an evil way, but as part of teaching her right from wrong, I sometimes resort to sitting her on a "time-out" chair. I thus provide a break in her thinking and try to re-direct her energy at the end of the designated time.

During one such time recently, we both needed "time out." Maria had hit me on the head with one of her toys and worse than the physical pain was the emotional pain of watching her enjoy the fact that I was hurt! I told her angrily that she had to stay on her chair until she was ready to tell me she was sorry.

Her giggles eventually gave way to tears as she realized I was serious. I'll never know if fear of rotting in the chair or repentance was the cause for her apology, but my heart melted when I heard her say, "I'm sorry, Mommy." We hugged each other and the incident was over.

Amazed at how fast I could feel my anger turning into forgiveness, I realized it was a God-given attribute. Humanly, it didn't make sense. Sometimes I choose to hang onto my anger when another person hurts me. I want to make them suffer for what I went through. But my mother-response to Maria's tears is surely more God-like.

When I persist in either giggling in the face of wrong, or being content if I am out of step with God, I cannot be forgiven. I am left to discover the loneliness of not being sorry.

When I recognize my need for renewed relationship, however, I can imagine the heart of God melting. It is then that I know my Forgiver.

JULY 23   Read Psalm 32

Imagine that you are a small child again, sitting on a "time-out" chair because of something you have done wrong. Read again the first two verses of this Psalm, imagining Jesus helping you get off your chair, hugging you, and playing another game with you.

JULY 24   Read Luke 7:36-50

Imagine that your mortgage, school loan, car loan, or other debt were suddenly paid off for you. Feel the surprise and relief it would be. Now think about all the pain and guilt from which Christ has either saved you or forgiven you. Hear the words of Jesus spoken to you personally, "Your sins are forgiven. Go in peace."

JULY 25   Read Jeremiah 31:10-17

For what child do you weep—either a nameless one or one you know? Pray for this child and its parents, that their tears will flow into the hope of Christ.

JULY 26   Read Isaiah 25:1-9

Close your eyes and admit your powerlessness to save yourself or to go through life alone. Then watch Jesus approach you and accept a brightly wrapped package from Him. Slowly unwrap it and look inside. What is it? What will you do with it? Respond to Jesus before you open your eyes again.

JULY 27   Read Matthew 6:14, 15

Think of a person who has hurt you and whom you cannot seem to forgive or even want to forgive. Separate your anger from your God-given ability to forgive and put them in two different boxes. Imagine giving the box with anger in it to Jesus, who receives it, and then goes on to help you deliver the box containing forgiveness to the other person.

JULY 28   Read Lamentations 2:11-19

Join the writer in writing a prayer of lament for the children of God who are crying today. Imagine Jesus crying with all of you, and then watch as He wipes the face of each and comes finally to you as well. Receive His cleansing and love.

JULY 29   Read II Corinthians 2:1-11

Think of the community to which you belong—either your local body of believers or a scattered group from which you receive support. Thank God, your ultimate Forgiver, for those persons through whom you receive that forgiveness in concrete ways.

Father

When John and I first met, we were classmates in college. We had fun together in the same circle of friends, but no sparks lit between us. I was surprised, therefore, when several years after college, and after losing track of him, I heard John's voice on the telephone. His father had died recently, and he called to talk. During that long conversation, he allowed me to share his tears of shock, emptiness, and pain.

We kept in touch after that and began to value our relationship more and more. Once, when I tested the waters to see how permanent this might become, I asked John if he thought a father-in-law could ever take the place of his father. "No one will ever replace my father," he said, "but I could probably benefit from having another father figure." My hope that it would be my father has come true; John and he love and respect each other in a father-son relationship.

Through John's experience of his father dying, I have learned more about the pain of that loss in many people's lives. I have also become aware of those who have never met their fathers, of those whose fathers don't love them, and of those who have been severely abused by the one who fathered them. I have been blessed with a wonderful father, yet I, too, by experiencing other father figures gain a fuller vision of the One Jesus called Father.

JULY 30   **Read Psalm 103**

What is the characteristic of God you most need to hear in this passage for today? Read that verse several times, letting its truth sink deeper and deeper into the center of your being.

JULY 31   **Read Malachi 2:10-17**

Look at each person you see today as your brother or sister in the Fatherhood of God. Notice how that attitude changes how you see people.

AUGUST 1   **Read John 14:1-14**

Give yourself permission to spend time contemplating the mystery of these verses. Jesus and God are One, your Father. Listen to your Father repeat the first verse to you, "Do not let your heart be troubled."

AUGUST 2   **Read Isaiah 64:8**

Into what kind of a pot are you being shaped? Can you trust yourself to be molded by this Father Potter who sees the broad, far-reaching picture of your beauty and usefulness?

AUGUST 3   **Read Luke 15:11-32**

In which character of this story do you see yourself? Imagine yourself as that person. Then reflect on how the father in the story portrays God to you in your present situation.

AUGUST 4   **Read Isaiah 65:17-25**

Read this as the description of what the perfect Father wants to give His children. Know that God wants this for you. Write a letter of response.

AUGUST 5   **Read Psalm 68:1-10**

Ask your Father God to help you forgive your human father for one of his imperfections.

GOD
of Our
Thirst

Deliverer

One of the mottos adopted by member of Alcoholics Anonymous (A.A.) is "One Day at a Time." They have even made bumper stickers out of that phrase to remind themselves and others that they only need to live one day at a time.

In the A.A. organization, the goal is to live one more day without drinking any alcohol. For members to plan to abstain for the rest of their lives is too overwhelming, after drinking so habitually and for so long, so they make their goal more manageable—one more day.

Jesus' disciples must have lived with a similar motto. Many times Jesus' teaching must have been confusing. His followers thought they had finally figured out his mission—to restore the kingdom to Israel. But when they asked him about it, supposing they would be the key helpers in this victory, Jesus told them they didn't need to know the details. He said, "It is not for you to know the times or dates" (Acts 1:7).

I, too, often thirst for more details. When will I find what I really want? How long will it last? What is God's will on this decision? I can easily become addicted to my own ways of thinking and behaving and wanting to know. I need God's power to deliver me from this self-centeredness, as well as to help me find freedom in the fact that I only need to live one day at a time. Like those in A.A., I can acknowledge my thirst for more knowledge, power, time, or whatever it is that I want, but also trust God to be my ultimate Deliverer, one day at a time.

AUGUST 6   Read Psalm 107:1-22

For what are you hungering and thirsting? Claim the promise of verse 9, pondering how God is satisfying your thirst. With what good things are you being filled? Close your time with your Deliverer with one of the suggestions in verses 21 and 22.

AUGUST 7   Read Matthew 5:1-6

What is the meaning, for you, of hungering and thirsting for righteousness? Depending on where your spiritual energy lies today, either pray for a renewed desire for this kind of hunger and thirst, or thank God for how you are being filled.

AUGUST 8   Read Revelation 7:13-17

Think of someone for whom you can make one of these promises of eternal life a reality for today, either by helping them spiritually or physically. It doesn't have to be a major gesture, but do it with the consciousness of sharing in God's great act of deliverance.

AUGUST 9   Read John 7:37

Close your eyes and imagine yourself at the end of a party you would be likely to attend. What part of you remains "empty" even after joining in the food, drink, friendship, and laughter the party had to offer? Then imagine Jesus asking you personally to come to Him so He can fill that emptiness. What does He say to do? What is your response? Write about the experience in your journal.

AUGUST 10 Read Judges 7:1-23

Who or what are the "troops" with which you are surrounded? Do you have so many that, like Gideon, it is hard to know when it is God helping you and when you are living on your own strength? Ask for the wisdom and humility to pare down your own "troops" so that God can be your obvious Deliverer.

AUGUST 11 Read Romans 14:13-19

Notice the difference in tone from yesterday's story in the Old Testament. Jesus has brought a new way—righteousness, peace, and joy—rather than killing revenge. Pray that God's peace and joy will come to nations that are presently attempting to use violence to solve their problems.

AUGUST 12 Read I Kings 19:1-9

Like Elijah, take a few moments to eat and drink of God's love. Let yourself be filled with the strength you will need for your impending journey. Let God be your preventive Deliverer.

Life-giver

When I was growing up, our family lived on a small farm just big enough to keep a few animals. We had a shed for rabbits, another shed for chickens, and a small barn for about 20 sheep.

One of my favorite times of the year was spring. Not only was the world of flowers and trees and creeks coming back to life, but the animals were more lively as well. The lambs especially were full of life, kicking and jumping and running all over the meadow. They still depended on their mothers for milk, but they flaunted an increasing independence as their wobbly legs strengthened.

Spring was also a celebration of life for those lambs who had lived. Inevitably one or two ewes died while giving birth, making orphans out of two or three of the tiny lambs. Every winter we set up a big box in our basement, filled it with straw, and nursed the orphans there with tender loving care. We warmed milk for them and fed them out of a baby's bottle. Many times the tiny animals died, regardless of how hard we tried to keep them alive. But repeated failures never made us give up. In fact, we always gave those motherless lambs much more energy than the healthy ones. It made sense. They needed us more!

Those lambs, and the way we cared for them, help me understand Jesus a little better. He came to give new life to those who are oppressed. It makes sense. We need Him more!

AUGUST 13   Read Psalm 143

Imagine that you are the parched land the Psalmist describes. Let your need for water match your thirst for God's life-giving Spirit.

AUGUST 14   Read Judges 15:18-20

Samson did not censor his request for water when he discovered there was none. He simply told God what he needed and God miraculously split open the earth into a spring of water! Try to think of what you need from God today without deciding whether or not you think it's possible to attain. Review who God was to you yesterday and ask for that which you need today.

AUGUST 15   Read Isaiah 55:1-5

Write an R.S.V.P. letter to the One who has invited you to come, drink, and eat of abundant life. What do you imagine the table of abundant life holds? Why do you easily accept the invitation—or have a hard time deciding whether or not to go? Believe that the Lord your God, the Holy One of Israel, has glorified you.

AUGUST 16   Read Luke 16:19-31

In what area of your life do you dwell in a "comfortable house"? Where has God blessed you so that you have plenty to share with those who are less fortunate? Think of one way today to refresh another with what you have been given in abundance.

AUGUST 17   Read I Corinthians 3:5-9

Think back over the past year and make a list of the people whose lives you have "watered." Who have you nurtured by sharing God's love in various ways? Give thanks for the chance to be used by God in these life-giving ways.

AUGUST 18   Read I Kings 17:7-16

Think back over the past year and make a list of the people whose lives have "watered" your own. Who has nurtured your love and thirst for God and shown you God's love ever more clearly? Thank God for each of these persons.

AUGUST 19   Read Revelation 22:17

What has this gift of the water of life meant to you this week? How have you been enriched personally? How have you seen your family life enriched? How have you noticed the earth being enriched because of God's life-giving love poured out for all?

Sacrifice

Some time ago I set out to accomplish one of the biggest dreams of my life. I spent my savings, packed up all my possessions, said good-bye to many friends, and moved 1,200 miles to a new land of hopes, dreams, and expectations.

Before too long, however, I clearly sensed God calling me to leave this "promised land" and move on to something else. Not knowing what that something else was to be, I became overwhelmed with the loss of what I was giving up. I felt like I was dying to my expectations and sacrificing my dreams. I resisted the change that was too soon, in my timing, and yet I eventually knew I had to do it.

Fortunately, throughout the entire experience I had a strong sense of God's presence. God was crying with me, but was also the strong one, saying, "Come on, I have even more to show you!" God gave me the strength to let part of me die so that I could find new life in moving on.

I felt, too, that I was more closely in touch than before with Jesus' sacrificial experience of giving up this life for much more. Jesus was born to die so that my life can be rich and full and meaningful—not only sometime later in heaven, but also right now. That doesn't mean I won't have times of dryness and feelings of being asked to sacrifice too much. Those become, in fact, the very times that I am able to see most clearly my inability to satisfy my own thirst, and I can watch Jesus, the ultimate Sacrifice, come to life again.

AUGUST 20   Read Psalm 22:1-18

This is a Good Friday Psalm. Stop with the verse that speaks to an experience you have had. Think about how it feels to know Jesus understands your suffering and/or sacrifice.

AUGUST 21   Read Esther 4

Plan to fast for at least one meal in the next few days. Let your hunger and thirst be a sacrificial reminder of others, who, like Esther, have fasted for spiritual purposes before you. Remember, too, the One who sacrificed His life so your life can be enriched. Use the time to write a letter of thanksgiving to this Jesus.

AUGUST 22   Read Acts 9:1-19

Even though Saul's fast was not consciously for spiritual purposes, God used this time to change his heart and his entire life-style. God used the strengths Saul was directing against the church to build a strong leader for the church. Pray for a leader who comes to your mind today, that his or her abilities will also be used by God to strengthen the church of Jesus Christ.

AUGUST 23   Read II Samuel 23:13-17

For whom in your life are you willing to make a sacrifice? Perhaps you will give an anonymous gift that you would really like for yourself. Maybe you will take someone else's turn at washing the dishes without keeping a record of it. Let your deed be a reminder to you of the unselfish sacrifice Jesus makes for you continually in love, forgiveness, and acceptance.

AUGUST 24   Read II Timothy 4:6-8

Imagine yourself, like Paul, knowing you are at the end of your life. Are the sacrifices you are presently making, the ones that you will look back on as being worthwhile? Pray for wisdom to make the right sacrifices. Pray for the strength to give willingly, even though you may sometimes feel that you are being poured out like a "drink offering."

AUGUST 25   Read II Corinthians 11:24-30

It is easy to complain of the sacrifices I am called upon to make without thinking of the many which I have never needed to make. Thank God today for all the hardships that have been kept from you. Meditate on the freedom and beauty in your life.

Close your eyes and let scenes from Jesus' life and death and resurrection flow through your mind. What part of Him would you most like to emulate? Ask for the grace and courage to have this thirst filled in you.

Hope

S tudies done on victims of concentration camps show that it is those with memories of happy family times who survived the longest. These people were also sustained by the hope that they would eventually be able to enjoy family times again. Those without memories or hope died.

Similarly, survival skills have been shown to be stronger in those victims of childhood abuse who have had at least one significant adult who listened to them and believed their story. Those who have had no such adult support lose hope in their struggle, and their development is considerably more damaged by the experience.

Fortunately, most people don't experience such drastic devastations, but everyone knows what it is to be in danger of losing hope, if only for a short time. Failing an important test, receiving a rejection letter, experiencing a cutting remark from one I love, or having too many rainy days in a row can allow feelings of worthlessness to rise to the top and take over my self-image. In these less traumatic times, as well as more violent ones, my hope is restored most quickly when I can remember good experiences of the past: tests I have passed, projects that were accepted, loving remarks I have received, and days of sunshine. Those memories also strengthen my hope that good times will come again.

God is my hope in the same sense. I read stories of others being nourished in their thirst for God. I have memories of God quenching my own thirst. And I have the promise that God will continue to offer that nourishment to me in the future as well. There will certainly be dry times, but always surrounded by my true Hope.

AUGUST 27   Read Psalm 42:1-6

Draw a picture of yourself as a deer looking for water. What does the water represent; for what does your soul long? Draw and label the water, and imagine it quenching your thirst.

AUGUST 28   Read Mark 9:38-41

Give yourself a cup of water to drink. Let it be a reminder of God filling you with health and hope.

AUGUST 29   Read Romans 5:1-5

Draw a tower in your journal of the elements in verse 3 that lead to hope. Beside each write an example of it from your life. Surround the entire tower with God's love and let the truth of your picture sink into your heart.

AUGUST 30   Read Romans 15:13

Pray this verse for three persons whom God brings to your mind.

AUGUST 31   Read Psalm 130

Quiet yourself with the patience of one who quietly waits for the morning. Slowly let yourself realize that when the sky lightens you are hoping to see God. What word of hope is God bringing to you? Receive it like a refreshing drink after a long night.

SEPTEMBER 1   Read Genesis 21:1-21

Notice how God met the needs of Hagar and Ishmael in a seemingly hopeless situation. Let yourself be filled with hope that this same God is still present to take care of your personal needs today.

SEPTEMBER 2   Read I Peter 1:3-9

Let the joy of knowing this Living Hope splash out on the people you meet today, like the extra water that splashes past your mouth when you drink from a water fountain!

GOD
of the
Seashore

Omnipresent

*T*hree days after my vacation at the beach, I continued to be reminded of its return home with me. Sand greeted me from the floor of the car every time I opened the door. It covered the floor of the shed where I stored the beach chairs. It stuck to the seashells in their new home on the dresser.

This was not much sand, however, compared to what we had lived with during five days of tenting on the dunes. We brushed it off as much as possible before crawling into our sleeping bags at night, but sand was simply part of life at the beach. We lay on it, covered ourselves in it, walked for miles on it, and watched it swirl in and out with the tides. It was normal there.

While at the beach, and then back home again, I marvel at the vastness of the seashore. To count the grains of sand on which I stood was impossible; to number the grains in sight was unfathomable; to know that this was but a tiny part of all the sand in the world was overwhelming!

In Psalm 139 the writer compares God's thoughts to the numbers of sand. This is a God who is everywhere, in every thought, at all times, and who cares more for me than I know of myself! This is the God of the Seashore and the God who has come home with me as well. This is the God who knew me before I was formed and knows what I will choose tomorrow. This is the God who knows no beginning and foresees no end. I am one of those many, but valuable, grains of sand to whom God is always present.

SEPTEMBER 3   Read Psalm 139

Spend five to ten minutes in silence, thinking about the goodness of God. Don't ask for anything; just offer praise for who God is.

SEPTEMBER 4   Read Psalm 121

Meditate on a picture of a mountain or on a memory you have of being surrounded by mountains. Imagine God's strength and help upholding, surrounding, and towering over you. Let this Omnipresence receive your fears of the day ahead.

SEPTEMBER 5   Read Matthew 13:33

Instead of imaging your smallness in comparison to the mountains you pictured yesterday, imagine yourself as a package of yeast that is small and has a great potential for growth. Who or what contributes to the moisture and warmth that mix with your life to help you grow? Thank God for these gifts.

SEPTEMBER 6   Read Matthew 10:26-31

Let each time you see your hair in the mirror, or each time you fix it today, be a reminder of how much God knows you and loves you.

SEPTEMBER 7   Read Acts 17:22-28

Close your eyes, relax, and rest your hands, palms up, imagining that you are on the seashore. Become aware of your breathing and let Paul's words become part of your rhythmic heartbeat, "God is not far from me."

SEPTEMBER 8   Read Ephesians 1:15-23

See the world today as being filled with God, as the seashore is covered with endless sand. God is everywhere, in everyone, awaiting your recognition. Breathe a prayer of thanks each time you see, hear, feel, touch, or taste a reminder of God.

SEPTEMBER 9   Read Hebrews 2:10-18

If today were to be your last one as you know life now, what would you do differently? Let your ever-present God, who cares about every detail of your life, help plan your day.

Lord

"What's new in your life?" The question came from my sister-in-law of eight years. Living 200 miles apart, we saw each other only two or three times a year.

It was a fun question to answer! I felt warmed by her interest in me and that she didn't assume I was doing all the same things and thinking all the same thoughts I had told her about six months earlier, when we had last been together.

Remembering how I liked being asked that, I have since asked other relatives and friends similar questions after being separated for some time. I am often surprised by how many new things they talk about, that I was not expecting. I am fascinated by how lives change and energies are re-directed in relatively short amounts of time. As I look at others, I see beauty in their flexibility and the variety of activities and feelings and stages they live through.

I find it much harder to recognize beauty in my own flexibility and change. I long for stability. I want to know my future. I want to be in control!

It's helpful when I can step outside myself and look at my life as the life of another or as the sand on the shore of the ocean. The beach is constantly remolded and reshaped by the tides, the winds, and the changing weather. Ocean waves carry part of the shore with them at each retreat and deposit a fresh design upon return. New arrangements of beauty are displayed all throughout the day at the seashore.

It is the Creative Lord of the seashore who also longs to help create and shape my life. I can be assured that this Lord will only enhance my life into more beauty than I could dream of doing alone.

SEPTEMBER 10 Read Psalm 63

Close your eyes and imagine yourself as the seashore with the waves of God's Lordship sweeping over you in a soothing and refreshing rhythm. Repeat the first phrase or verse of this Psalm over and over, acknowledging your thirst for God and your desire to be shaped by this One who loves you more than any other does.

SEPTEMBER 11 Read Genesis 22:15-18

Imagine yourself as one of these spiritual descendants of Abraham, lying on the seashore with many other grains of sand from throughout the ages. Unending gifts await those who choose to follow and love God. Rejoice!

SEPTEMBER 12 Read Joshua 11:1-9

Think of a group of people of which you are not a part, that seem as numerous as the sand on the seashore. Write in your journal how it feels to be part of a minority. Know that God stands with you, ready to protect you. Let your Lord assure you of the importance of your individual grain-like life!

SEPTEMBER 13   Read Psalm 97

Do a word association with "Lord," by paying attention to the feelings and words that come to you when you hear the word. The number of positive or negative connotations you associate with "Lord" may affect your willingness to see God as your Lord. Ask for an ever increasing desire to live out the command in verse 12.

SEPTEMBER 14   Read Matthew 10:46-52

If you were to call out, "Jesus, have mercy on me," to what would you be referring? Imagine Jesus coming to your side, not to zap you with answers, but to help you discover your answer to His question, "What do you want me to do for you?" Talk or write to this Lord.

SEPTEMBER 15   Read Isaiah 45:18-25

Think of a person in your life who has helped you see the Lordship of God as portrayed in this passage—creator of love, truth, right living, strength, and all good things. Offer a special prayer of thanksgiving for this person.

SEPTEMBER 16   **Read John 21:1-12**

How do others recognize the Lord in your life? How do you see
the Lord at work in your community or alive in the world? What
is your life's version of standing on the seashore and watching a
"big catch" come in?

Giver of Gifts

A s I watched children playing on the beach, I decided to join
the fun. I began to dig a hole in the sand, but as the hole
grew bigger, I began to feel empty inside.

Suddenly a little boy came by and silently dumped a pail of
water into the hole. His act seemed to be a symbol of God's gifts
coming to me, filling my emptiness. As the child repeatedly went
back for more water, I continued digging, no longer creating
emptiness, but, instead, a place to receive whatever he brought to
me.

As the boy eventually ran off to find another playmate, I
watched the water slowly disappear into the walls of the hole. I
realized that I want to let God's gifts do the same thing in my
life—seep in and move on to those around me.

I continued to think about God as my Giver of gifts while the
day turned into late afternoon and I began to walk along the beach.
I suddenly noticed a scurrying movement at my feet. Hundreds
of tiny white crabs were running sideways in all directions,

disappearing quickly into the sand as I approached!

I also noticed many seashells, algae, and other debris the waves had washed up and abandoned on the beach. I stuffed my pockets with the prettiest.

Other places appeared to be stretches of smooth sand, but I discovered them to be treasure beds of rocks and shells when I did a little digging. The beach gave up its "treasures" freely. It seemed full, waiting to share with anyone who took the time and had the interest to collect from its huge storehouse.

I realize that I, too, am a storehouse for God's treasures. I have been given love, forgiveness, friends, the earth, and much more. When I recognize the supply of time, energy, and compassion which I have been given, I enjoy life more and am also more free to imitate God, my Giver of many gifts.

SEPTEMBER 17   **Read Psalm 86**

Which part of the Psalmist's prayer is true for your life? Spend time with the phrase or verse with which you most easily identify, receiving it as a gift anew this moment.

SEPTEMBER 18   **Read Genesis 41:41-57**

What is a current struggle or hardship in your life that could be used by God as a gift? Listen to the wandering of your thoughts.

SEPTEMBER 19   Read John 15:1-8

Think of your life as a beach containing many treasures—some visible for any passerby, some just below the surface, and others hidden deeply inside. What are your treasures? Pick up several of them for a closer look. Be aware of the One to whom you are connected and Who nourishes you to grow stronger. Claim the promise of verse 7.

SEPTEMBER 20   Read Matthew 25:14-30

What is a gift God has entrusted to your care, for use in this world? Write God a letter of appreciation and ask how you can use it to be of further service.

SEPTEMBER 21   Read Genesis 1:26-31

Imagine being in the garden and having God come to you, saying, "This is very good." Can you believe this for yourself? Believe it as God's value judgment, especially for the parts of yourself you find hard to accept.

SEPTEMBER 22   Read Galatians 5:22-26

All followers of Christ are given each fruit of the Spirit as a free gift of membership. What fruit of the Spirit has been most evident in your life this week? Which one needs more practice? In what ways are the others evident in your life?

SEPTEMBER 23   **Read Matthew 10:5-10**

Imagine that you are one of the original twelve apostles. What gifts has God deposited into your life like gifts of the sea, that give you the authority to be a witness for Jesus as your Ultimate Giver of gifts?

Wisdom

I watched absentmindedly as the two children in front of me on the beach built a castle in the sand. When I awoke later, they were still hard at work, making roads around it, sloppily carrying water from the ocean to fill the trenches, poking sticks in the mounds to serve as flagpoles.

Didn't they know they were too close to the water? All their hard work would be washed away in a few hours. I went back to sleep.

When I returned the following day, sure enough, no signs remained of the children's creations. Their laughter and joy-filled busyness, however, lingered in the air and in my memory of that spot. Maybe they, being children, didn't care if their project had disappeared. Maybe they were having so much fun with the process that the end result didn't matter much. Maybe they had used their time more wisely than I had with my naps! I have a lot to learn about trusting and enjoying life as it comes.

Maybe what I need to do is unlearn some of my adult "wisdom." Now that I have learned something about living as a responsible adult, I try to laugh more quietly and not cry at all, at least in public. When I fall, I'm embarrassed all day, rather than jumping up and hurrying on to the next adventure. I have worked hard at controlling my emotions. I have learned a lot about "adult" behavior and about how to live up to the expectations of others.

I wonder if I have become too practical to understand what wisdom is. Lord, have mercy.

SEPTEMBER 24   **Read Psalm 111**

Find a comfortable position. Relax. Ponder the works of the Lord. Can you delight in what God is doing in your life, whether or not you are living up to other's expectations? You are unique and will hear God's unique words to you as you take time to listen for yourself.

SEPTEMBER 25   **Read I Kings 4:29-34**

Wisdom was a gift to Solomon from God. Is it your desire to grow in the wisdom of God? Take time to study a tree or animal today. Ask God to show you what Solomon might have said, from his wealth of wisdom about this tree or animal. You, too, can ask for this wisdom.

SEPTEMBER 26 — Read Exodus 1:22-2:10

Going against this law of the land was recorded as an act of wisdom by the Scripture writers. What in your Christian convictions goes against the popular beliefs or laws of your land? Ask God for wisdom, courage, and continuing direction to live against the flow when the flow is not with the God of Wisdom.

SEPTEMBER 27 — Read Colossians 1:9-14

Plan time in your busyness today to play like a child building a sand castle—not for production's sake, but for pleasure in this life God has given you. Maybe this, too, can be a way for you to grow in the knowledge of God!

SEPTEMBER 28 — Read Psalm 119:97-104

Is there a commandment of God that seems more burdensome than edifying? Ask to understand God's wisdom in giving this commandment, so that it will become sweeter than honey to you, rather than just a hard precept to obey.

SEPTEMBER 29 — Read Colossians 1:24-29

Rather than focusing on your gaining in wisdom, focus today on the mystery of Christ in you. Image yourself with Christ, like the ocean and seashore existing together. You can't know where one begins and the other ends because they interact so fully with each other.

SEPTEMBER 30   **Read I Corinthians 3:18-23**

Pray for the leaders of the nations, of your country, of your community, and of your church, that they will bypass the wisdom of this world for the true Wisdom of God. Think, too, of the areas of your own leadership. Pray that the wisdom of God will enter every thought and decision you make in this line of duty.

GOD
of the
Clouds

Creator

My earliest memory of awakening to the amazing world God created is from an afternoon when I was four years old. I was playing in the snow with my neighbors. We were all lying on our backs in the fresh layer of cold, powdery white snow, flapping our arms and legs in wide semi-circles to make our imprints as snow angels.

In that position, looking up into the sky, I made an incredible discovery—the clouds were moving! I was both terrified and exhilarated. Part of the stability of my young life was floating away, right before my eyes. I felt unsure of anything. What if the ground, too, would begin to tremble and the trees I climbed walk away?

While I was scared, I was also thrilled. I felt like there was so much to be explored and enjoyed! From then on I spent hours lying on my back, watching the moving clouds.

Clouds have come to symbolize for me that I share in creating and that God continues to create. By creating the clouds, God made a way to create anew each day. Wispy cotton-candy clouds. Huge exploding puffs that tumble over each other. The menacing darkness of impending rain.

Clouds always seem to be busy in their play, waiting for us to join them in praise of our mutual Creator.

OCTOBER 1   **Read Psalm 148**

Lie on your back looking up into the sky. Imagine all of creation around, beneath, and above you joining you in praise to the Lord. What calls you to praise today?

OCTOBER 2   Read Genesis 1:6-8

Imagine yourself joining God in the second day of creating the world. Watch the waters separate into lakes and streams, seas below and clouds above. Believe that God's act of creation is happening again today. Rest in the security of this amazing Creator who is yours as well!

OCTOBER 3   Read Genesis 9:8-17

Color a rainbow in your journal. Add a prayer of thanksgiving to go with this symbol of God's covenant to you. Color another rainbow to give to another person as a shared reminder of God's promised presence.

OCTOBER 4   Read Job 36:22-33

Spend time today looking for pictures and shapes in the clouds. Notice their changes throughout the day, letting them be a reminder to you of God's creating power. Be a co-creator by producing an attitude of praise within yourself.

OCTOBER 5   Read Colossians 1:15-20

Sit in silence for ten minutes, taking a mental walk through the day that lies ahead. Be thankful for each person and place and thing you see that you know is created by God. Don't forget to look up to notice the clouds!

OCTOBER 6   **Read Ecclesiastes 11:3-5**

We have come to understand and predict some parts of creation. Meditate on one aspect of God's creation which continues to baffle you, predictable or not. End your prayer with a written response to God.

OCTOBER 7   **Read Psalm 104**

A Psalm of creation! What part of creation most fills you with awe for your Creator? Stop in the correlating verse. Let God's splendor seep into the center of your being and then expand to engulf all of you.

Sustainer

*I*f the clouds won't supply the earth with rain, we turn on the sprinkler so our lawn doesn't dry up.

If we're in a financial crunch, we get another job or work harder for a raise.

If we're hungry, we go to the refrigerator or stop at a fast-food restaurant along the way.

In our affluent way of life, it's easy to forget that God is our sustainer. It's easier to recognize that we depend on our cars, friends, money, clothes and jobs. To a certain extent, we feel like we can control those things. We see them in a tangible way, which makes them seem worthy of our trust.

Sometimes I wish I were a tree or a bird—totally dependent on God for my sustenance, without being tempted to look to other things. I see a cloud floating past the window where I'm hard at work and long to be free-floating, like they are.

If I were stripped of control over my life, however, like a cloud, I wouldn't have the gift of a relationship with my Sustainer. I wouldn't know anything of God's love. I wouldn't have the intellectual ability to know that God exists.

So in the end, I need to put more energy into my desire to be in relationship with God, simply accepting and returning God's love. My intellect frees me to understand that I cannot put my faith in my possessions or reputation. How strange that I often bypass the only true Sustainer to trust in the temporary providers of sustenance. I need God's courage to bypass the security of the possessions I can see, for the sustenance of God that may be less apparent, at least initially.

OCTOBER 8   Read Psalm 147:1-11

Pray for a greater sense throughout this week of your dependence on God. Add a verse to this Psalm about one thing you have seen in your life that comes from God. Hold the promise of verse 11 in your heart as your highest calling in life.

OCTOBER 9   Read Exodus 13:17-22

God, in great wisdom and with foresight beyond our immediate desires, guides us, too, on the best path for our lives. What is the "pillar of cloud" (or promised guidance) that sustains you on today's journey? Write it down and let the clouds be a reminder of the promise throughout the day.

OCTOBER 10   Read 1 Corinthians 10:1-4

Make a list of those material things on which you depend. Can you see them as part of the spiritual rock that you've been given to help you know God's sustaining power in a deeper way?

OCTOBER 11   Read 1 Thessalonians 4:13-18

Make a list of the people on whom you've come to depend. Part of God's gift as Sustainer is to give us the presence of other believers who can encourage us now. Give a word of encouragement to a Christian brother or sister today.

OCTOBER 12   Read Psalm 99

God answers those who are willing to ask and to listen, not only Moses and Aaron, but we who live today as well. Let the thoughts and worries that fill your mind float up into the clouds as an offering to God. Imagine God catching them. What is God's response to you?

OCTOBER 13   **Read Job 26**

Listen to a piece of music that lifts you up to feel God's loving presence within and surrounding you. Through the music let yourself relax and be loved by God, as if floating on the clouds.

OCTOBER 14   **Read Luke 12:54-56**

What does Jesus mean by the question, "How is it that you don't know how to interpret this present time?" How is He asking you to look at what you see in your world today?

Refuge

*E*ver since my first airplane flight my favorite part of the trip has been flying through the clouds, and then just over the clouds, as if floating along on a fluffy pillow. I have a sense of security, as though the clouds will hold me up and shield me from all the problems and worries I had on the earth!

We all know that flying above the clouds lacks any reality of safety. We've learned to discriminate whether something is truly a refuge, and to know, for the most part, what is or is not safe.

We know that when we go out walking on a dark city street at night, we are not necessarily safe, even when we see no one who can harm us. We're aware that not everyone in our world has enough food, even though we don't see gaunt faces of the starving looking through our windows while we eat. We've learned that the sun's rays can burn our skin, even when it's hidden from our sight behind the clouds.

Even though we've learned, in some cases, to differentiate between truth and what only appears to be truth, we tend to prefer living with illusions of our safety than to think about how little control we really have. We build fences, secure alarm systems, and lock our doors. We can get so busy taking care of ourselves that we forget that God is our only real Refuge.

I have never known the kind of total dependence on God as I saw lived by the refugees of El Salvador. Stripped of their homes, crops, and sometimes even their families, they carried no pretentions of their lives being secure. They received each moment as a gift. God really was their ultimate and only Refuge. Sometimes I wonder if all my securities, false or partial though they may be, keep me from knowing my need of God as fully as I ought.

Lord, please forgive.

OCTOBER 15   **Read Psalm 91**

Substitute "you" for "he" and "him" in verses 14-16, receiving it as God's personal promise to you. God is your refuge, not because of anything you have done to deserve it, but because of your love for God and God's love for you. It is beyond what our human minds can conceive! Ask God to give you the ability to receive this great Refuge.

OCTOBER 16   Read Numbers 35:9-15

Spend time looking at the clouds, either in the sky or in a picture of clouds. Ask God to bring to mind something you've thought or done that needs to be forgiven. Imagine the clouds being your cities of refuge. Go there in your mind to get away and talk with God about your sin. In closing, receive God's forgiveness and courage to go on.

OCTOBER 17   Read Acts 1:6-11

As you observe the clouds today, imagine them as enveloping Jesus' presence. Be thankful that He not only went up into the clouds, but remains with you as your Refuge as well.

OCTOBER 18   Read Psalm 142

What part of your life is imprisoned? Are you seeking your own release, or can you let God be your Refuge? Rewrite this Psalm as your own cry for help. Include your specific needs and acknowledge the truth of verse 5.

OCTOBER 19   Read Joel 3:14-21

Which of your friends is presently in a "valley of decision"? Send them a note with the promises you find in Joel 3:14-21.

OCTOBER 20   Read Matthew 11:27-30

Close your eyes and imagine yourself melting into your chair until you are totally relaxed. Let Jesus come to you, giving you permission to rest for a few moments. Enjoy Jesus' presence and love, and let the silence be your prayer.

OCTOBER 21   Read Deuteronomy 33:24-29

What are the gates and shields you have erected around yourself for safety? God comes to you with the promise of holding you in everlasting arms and being your strong Refuge. Let God replace your bars with arms of protection and love.

GOD
of Our
Baptism

Simplicity

A few weeks ago I attended an extraordinary baptismal service. It was not unusual in its grandeur and ceremony, but rather in its simplicity. A small crowd gathered under the trees in the pastor's yard that Sunday evening to witness and celebrate with Leota, a 70-year-old woman, who wanted to publicly confess her faith in Jesus Christ.

After we worshiped together in song and other prayer, Leota shared with us a little of her story, both her life before she knew Jesus, and the freedom and joy she had experienced since deciding to become a believer. Several people then helped her into the pastor's swimming pool, where she was baptized. I had not met Leota previously, but as she told her story I recognized a oneness in Christ that brought us together as sisters.

Her age and ill health took away any magical qualities that one might associate with such an occasion. Leota's friends surrounded her, holding her glasses, being careful with her bad back, helping her with each step, standing by with a towel to wrap around her dripping body when she came out.

The informality of the service made me realize how simple our faith in Christ is. A heartfelt request, "I need Your help, God, to live this life You've given me," is enough. Never mind how sophisticated our words are to describe God, or how extraordinary our experience has been in realizing that we need God. All that matters is that we come, in love with Jesus, and ready to let that love relationship rule the rest of our lives. Leota expressed this simple joy well as she emerged from the water with the simple prayer, "Thank You, Jesus."

OCTOBER 22   Read Psalm 62

Let your soul find rest today in God alone, from whom your salvation comes. Thank God for Jesus' gift of salvation, and think about the difference that will make in your life this week.

OCTOBER 23   Read Mark 1:4-8

John the Baptist is witness to the fact that meaning in life does not come from an abundance of things. Ask God to show you how to simplify your life in order to live it more meaningfully. Are you prepared to hear God's answer?

OCTOBER 24   Read Matthew 3:1-6

Imagine yourself in this story as one of the people of Judea, coming out to receive the baptism John offers. What is the burden that lifts from your heart with this forgiveness? Accept Jesus' forgiveness for your sins again today.

OCTOBER 25   Read John 1:19-28

What responses would you have to these queries: "Who are you?" and "What do you say about yourself?" Does your life make others want to ask these kinds of questions? In your journal write out your answers and pray that God will lead you to people with whom you can share how Jesus makes a difference in your life.

OCTOBER 26   Read Acts 8:26-40

It's a miraculous story . . . or is it simply one of chance? How the eunuch interpreted this experience changed the course of his entire life. Do you see the day ahead of you as miraculous or open to chance? Your attitude may not change the circumstances, but it will change your day!

OCTOBER 27   Read Matthew 5:33-37

Keep track for one day how often you are tempted to elaborate on your "yes" or "no." Thank God for taking care of your reputation so you can practice simplicity in your speech, as well as in the rest of your life.

OCTOBER 28 **Read Matthew 19:13-15**

Imagine yourself as a child, sitting on Jesus' lap. Feel His hands on your head and receive His blessing. Know that the kingdom of heaven belongs to you.

Indwelling Spirit

"*I* don't know how to pray for him any more. We've been praying for him for years and it seems like he's as far as ever from letting God rule in his life!"

"This job is too big for me! I know God has called me to this place and I've agreed to the job, but it scares me to death. I don't see how I can supervise all these people when I've just begun to learn their way of life."

"God, please help me. I can't stand working with her one more day. I know you love her, but I sure don't see how!"

Can you remember the last time something similar has come out of your mouth, or maybe just crossed your mind? They are typical prayers of anyone who is trying to live in submission to God's direction. It is the prayer that sounds like we are at the end of our rope. Just because we have the desire to live like Jesus would, doesn't mean we always know how to do it. And often our first reaction to these predicaments is to work harder at finding an answer.

I have a feeling, however, that when God hears these claims

of exasperation, there is rejoicing in heaven! When we give up trying to do things on our own, the time is exactly right for us to realize that God has given us the Holy Spirit for that very reason.

In creating human beings, God planted the need and desire for something greater than ourselves within us. When we respond to that desire by accepting Christ as our Lord, we are made complete with the gift of the Holy Spirit, who intercedes for us.

We don't have to know how to pray.

We don't have to be able to do what we've been called to do.

We don't have to be able to love everyone on our own.

Admission of our weakness may be the best time for God's work to be done through us!

OCTOBER 29 Read Psalm 19

Read each verse slowly, thanking God for all these reasons why you don't have to be strong enough to do everything on your own. Be aware of the Holy Spirit within you, praising God beyond your words.

OCTOBER 30 Read John 3:1-15

Born again—it's become a familiar clichW1é. But what does it mean in your life? Make a list of the ways your life is different because you have Christ's Spirit dwelling within you and acting through you. Ask for God's help in an area you would like to give anew to the Spirit today.

OCTOBER 31 — Read Acts 1:1-5

Imagine that you are one of the apostles to whom Jesus gave instructions through the Holy Spirit before He was taken up to heaven. What proof does He continue to give to you that He is alive? Write to a nonbeliever, in your journal or in a letter, telling of your experience.

NOVEMBER 1 — Read John 14:15-21

Find a mirror for today's meditation. As you look into it, let it be a reminder of Christ's promise to live in you. Look into the eyes of others you see today and remind yourself that Christ is also in them.

NOVEMBER 2 — Read John 16:5-11

Sometimes it's hard to remember that the Comforter is even more present to us than Jesus was to His disciples. Choose a symbol of the Holy Spirit to carry with you for a day. Let it be a reminder of the Spirit's constant presence within you.

NOVEMBER 3 — Read Luke 17:20-21

Close your eyes, relax, and remember the water of your baptism flowing over you. Let its symbolism of new life in the Spirit seep into your pores and tantalize your senses. Feel and enjoy the life within!

Think of a person you have a hard time loving. Imagine that person being bathed in the baptism of Jesus' love. Remember Jesus' promise to be with you to the very end of the age, even in difficult relationships. How can you let Jesus' love "baptize" that person through you?

Holy

I wanted to go back and experience the day again. It had been so special—watching, hearing, and feeling the thrill of my best friend's baptism. We had sung and worshiped together, and I felt like we were joining all the saints from the ages before us in a huge chorus of blessing. As the Scriptures were read and as testimonies were given, I knew Jesus was in our midst. I saw the joy of the Holy Spirit descend on my friend as she came out of the water and as we all shared in the Lord's Supper. It was wonderful!

As I neared the edge of the lake again today, however, I felt drawn by a part of God I hadn't fully experienced in the din of yesterday's celebration. Alone now, the quietness around me became vivid.

The lake was hushed—no ripples or splashes of God's people entering and being enfolded in its bosom. A single bird's clear song replaced the crowded airways of my memories, filled with cries of joy, tears, and laughter. The wind was still now, too, and in the loud silence I was humbled in awe.

Yesterday I had been impressed by the simplicity of faith, by the ease with which any of us can be in relationship with God. I was also comforted by the fact that God's Spirit dwells within me. I never need to be alone or abandoned to my own strength. But there is another aspect of God that goes beyond my capacity to describe. It goes beyond my knowledge of who God is and my wildest imaginations of what God can do. It defies human understanding, because God is above all. God is holy.

All I can do in the face of my Holy God is to worship. I have no higher calling in life than to stand amazed in God's presence and praise who God is.

Praise God's holy name.

NOVEMBER 5   **Read Psalm 11**

"The Lord is in his holy temple." Repeat this verse over and over again as you kneel in awe and praise of God's holiness. Let the phrase become as natural in you as your breathing. End your quiet time with thanksgiving for the part of God that's beyond your comprehension.

NOVEMBER 6   **Read Matthew 3:11, 12**

Imagine yourself as a grain of wheat—one of many, and yet unique and distinguished from the chaff. What does it mean for you to be gathered into Jesus' barn?

NOVEMBER 7   Read John 1:29-34

Stand with John as Jesus walks toward him. Jesus is looking directly at you as He comes. Take time to notice what Jesus looks like, how He walks, what He wears, and what He does or says when He reaches you. Let yourself fully experience this man of holiness.

NOVEMBER 8   Read Matthew 6:5-13

Hallowed means holy. Stop after the first phrase of the Lord's prayer to contemplate what it means to call on God's holy name. Then notice how your attitude of honor affects the rest of the prayer.

NOVEMBER 9   Read Isaiah 48:17-21

Think back on your own life to how the Holy One of Israel has directed you, taught you what is best for you, given you peace like a river, and quenched your thirst in the deserts. Write a thank you note to your Holy God.

NOVEMBER 10   Read Revelation 4:6-11

Take a walk today and note all the things, animals, and people created by God. Memorize verse 11 to pray as you walk.

NOVEMBER 11   **Read I Peter 3:13-22**

Think again of the moment of your baptism. Since then you are connected with each other person who has become pledged to God through the symbol of water, ever since Noah and his family were saved through water! Like God's holiness, it is too much to perceive. Simply give thanks.

Light

I once belonged to a church which always seemed to be on the lookout for a good reason to celebrate. They specialized in having fun, laughing, and enjoying life. Everyone in town knew about that little church. It was like a giant candle, lighting all the individual candles who came there to worship. They in turn lit up everything and everyone around them with their spirit of joy. I considered them to be experts in the art of celebration.

Recently I received their newsletter and I wasn't surprised to read an announcement of another idea for how to celebrate! All members were to report to the church secretary the dates of their baptisms, so they could erect a big calendar with everyone's special day marked on it. Then they would brainstorm together on ways to celebrate their birthdays into the Christian faith, and the fun would begin!

Embarrassed, I realized that I couldn't even remember the date of my baptism! Besides that, I had never thought of it as an occasion to celebrate each year.

As I continued to read of their plans, however, I felt my excitement begin to ignite. I was already thinking of ways to celebrate the day. I had decided to let Jesus be my Light. Celebrating that day yearly seemed a fitting way to rekindle my memories of the light that came to live in me then, and to gain a fresh spark in my present life as well. It could be the kind of celebration that would be special not only to me, but could be a witness to those who haven't yet made that decision, a further light of encouragement.

Like my physical birth, baptism happens once in my life. But I hope my living out of that moment will continue to light my life and the lives of those around me.

NOVEMBER 12   **Read Psalm 4**

Can you remember the date of your baptism? If not, look through your records, write to the church where it took place, or ask someone who might know. Mark the day on your calendar and begin to make plans about how you can celebrate its anniversary. Re-light that day in your life!

NOVEMBER 13   **Read I John 1:5-10**

Close your eyes and imagine the light of Christ surrounding you, holding you, and keeping you warm. Your darkness is forgiven, and you, too, are part of the light. Give glow-ry to God in your praise and thanksgiving.

NOVEMBER 14   Read I John 2:7-11

Is hatred keeping you from experiencing the true light? No grudge is worth keeping, causing you to give up the peacefulness of God's light. Commit yourself to pray each day for a week that the light of God's goodness will shine on the person you haven't been able to love.

NOVEMBER 15   Read Luke 2:1-14

Jesus was born as Light to a world in which there was much fear. Jesus comes again today as Light. Name your fears to which you are willing to let Jesus bring light.

NOVEMBER 16   Read Matthew 5:14-16

We are not lit so that people will notice us, but so that God will be seen in us. Spend some time asking God to use you as a light on a hill today, and then go into your world with the confidence of God's grace shining into the life of each person you see.

NOVEMBER 17   Read Matthew 3:13-17

The "light of the world" was finally shown to all people. Find a picture of Jesus' baptism, or use one from your imagination, to enter this story into your meditation.

NOVEMBER 18   **Read John 1:1-18**

What are the blessings, one after another as verse 16 says, that you have received because of the light Christ brings to your life? Write the ones from this week in your journal.

GOD
of the
Sea

Awesome

I had only been at this spot three times before in my life, but I felt I was coming home. I climbed a huge rock that braved the repeated pounding of the Pacific Ocean, yet at the same time offered a soft respite of moss and plants on its gently sloping face. As I sank into the rock, watched the waves crash below, and listened to the deafening roar of the water, I no longer needed to figure out life and how I felt. I could just sit in the presence of the Almighty God, so evident here, and be.

One of my best friends had just died after a long struggle with cancer. I needed a place for my spirit to heal and was drawn to the ocean, as if my soul knew there was nothing else I could do. The last time I had come to celebrate an upcoming job transition to what I hoped would be a brighter future. The time before that I was reeling from having had a dream swept out from under my feet, leaving me confused and angry. And the first time had been on the blissful occasion of my honeymoon.

On each of my four visits to the Pacific, I had much the same experience. I was able to feel much more deeply, either the joy or the pain. The feeling, however, went beyond explosion or devastation. It was as if Someone were holding me and helping me absorb all the feelings. I wasn't overcome by them, and I didn't need words for them. Indeed, words were lost to me and I had no reason to try to find them. I found it enough to listen and watch the continuously pounding surf, to be and to feel and to know that their Creator, the Awesome God, would remain continuously with me as well.

NOVEMBER 19 Read Job 11:7-9

Close your eyes and imagine looking out over the ocean. Be aware of its size and power, its noise and rhythm. Let it be to you a symbol of the awesomeness of God that goes beyond words.

NOVEMBER 20 Read Psalm 66

The awesomeness of God calls forth praise for who God is, rather than thanksgiving for what God does. Let your prayer today be a psalm of adoration, as in verses 1-4.

NOVEMBER 21 Read Psalm 96

Think of an offering or gift that you could bring to the Lord. If you can, look into the eyes of God as you come. Let God, the Awesome, but also the One who loves you personally, receive your gift.

NOVEMBER 22 Read Habakkuk 2:14

Memorize this verse to repeat throughout the day. Let it surround your every thought and action as the ocean surrounds a fish.

NOVEMBER 23   Read Psalm 24

Live your day in the anticipation that at any moment the King of glory will come strolling through your neighborhood or work place. What are the signs that this Awesome One is already living there?

NOVEMBER 24   Read Isaiah 51:9-16

Sketch a series of pictures in your journal of the images you see as you read this passage. Then give yourself time to soak in the awesomeness of this God.

NOVEMBER 25   Read Psalm 89:5-18

Take a walk and notice the ways in which nature is praising the wonders of the Lord. Pray for the freedom to do so just as easily yourself.

Savior

As I anticipate and begin the season of Advent, I think of joy and happiness. I wait expectantly to celebrate Jesus' birthday, complete with all my individual, family, and church traditions.

I easily forget the feelings of fear and discouragement that must have been a part of that first Advent season. When the angel appeared to Zechariah, proclaiming the good news of a son to be born to him and Elizabeth, "he was startled and was gripped with fear" (Lk. 1:12). When the angel went to Mary to announce the Lord's special favor to her, "Mary was greatly troubled at his words" (Lk. 1:29).

What made all situations bearable was God's continual presence and reassurance. To Zechariah the angel said, "Do not be afraid." These words were repeated to Mary and to the shepherds. What began with startling terror was met with God's love and promise of good news of great joy, "Do not be afraid."

On my last trip to the ocean, I was reminded of a similar paradox. At one particular spot where the bay waters meet the ocean, people stood waist-deep all along the edge, fishing. These persons were gathering "food," next to a marker which listed the names of those whose lives had been claimed by these same waters. Waters of life had also dealt a terrifying blow of death!

God did not come in Jesus so that I could abandon my respect for the Holy, but because as a human being I cannot save myself. When I am most aware of God's awesomeness, I can most joyfully hear God's words, "Do not be afraid. I have sent you a Savior."

NOVEMBER 26   Read Psalm 95:1-8

Pray this song of worship and obedience on your knees as a symbol of your respect for the Holy One. End your prayer with a time of listening for the voice of God, to which verse 7 calls you.

NOVEMBER 27   Read Deuteronomy 30:11-20

Thank God for all your ancestors, either by blood or by faith who have chosen life with Christ, providing the example of love and obedience that nurtures your own relationship with Him. Imagine these gifts washing toward you from across time as the ocean rolls in from faraway lands.

NOVEMBER 28   Read Isaiah 57:14-21

Imagine that you are the ocean. Are you enjoying a steady rhythm or caught in the turbulent tossing? Humble your spirit and be reminded of the Savior you have in Christ. If a prayer of confession is what you have to offer today, end it in thanks for Christ's saving assurance of forgiveness.

NOVEMBER 29   Read Isaiah 11:10-16

Do you feel like there is an impassable ocean separating you from God? Reread verse 15 and imagine God blowing the sea apart

into many channels and making a way to cross. Don't work on
your relationship with God today. Just watch God's preparation
for you and anticipate what awaits you this Advent season.

NOVEMBER 30   Read I John 5:1-12

What new life are you hoping the birth of Jesus will bring to you
this season? Write a letter to the unborn baby, telling Him of your
needs and expectations.

DECEMBER 1   Read Psalm 98

Listen to a recording of your favorite Advent or Christmas song.
Turn up the volume and sing as though you are trying to compete
with the majesty and roar of the sea!

DECEMBER 2   Read John 3:16-21

This passage is a quote of Jesus'. Receive it as an early Christmas
gift from your Savior to take with you throughout the Advent
season.

Compassionate

As Christmas approaches, I think of my friends who are joyfully preparing for a child. They have been given a special sharing in that first season of waiting for Christ's birth, along with Mary and Joseph and Elizabeth and Zechariah. They are discovering what it feels like to wait for a child with excitement and joy.

Zechariah and Elizabeth were old enough to be grandparents, but still they had no children. On top of their own disappointment, they had further reason for sadness. In their time it was believed that if a couple did not have children, they were cut off from God. It was a sign that they were doing something wrong, and barrenness was God's punishment. That is likely what Zechariah was praying about as he was doing his job as a priest in the temple. He and Elizabeth followed all the commandments of God. Why would God keep children from them?

As we know in hindsight, God had a special reason for letting Elizabeth and Zechariah wait so long for a child. Elizabeth could then be proof to Mary that nothing is impossible with God. God's compassion for their situation was more clearly shown than if they had had a family according to normal timing.

God's compassion sometimes seems to ebb and flow in my life. Here today; gone tomorrow. I see only the edge of the ocean and the tidal changes seem drastic. God's view of my life, however, includes the entire ocean. What I see along the edges is merely a reminder that God is continually moving in my entire life. God's compassion never disappears, and my prayers, like Elizabeth's and Zechariah's, are heard.

DECEMBER 3   Read Luke 1:5-19

What is it that you are praying for in your life right now that hasn't been answered? Let the story of how God finally came to Zechariah and Elizabeth in such a miraculous way be a hope-filled story for your life too. Pray for patience to wait, to see the broader picture, and to be able to keep coming to God with all your desires, hopes, and expectations. Know that God also says to you, "I have heard your prayer."

DECEMBER 4   Read Psalm 77

Pray verses 11-15 again. Then write in your journal about one or two of the times during this past year that you have experienced God as compassionate.

DECEMBER 5   Read Micah 7:18-20

Close your eyes and imagine riding on a ship out into the ocean, so far you can no longer see the shore. With you is a bag of sins that you have been keenly aware of lately. One at a time, take them out and drop them over the side of the ship, letting the weight they have been to you carry them to the bottom of the ocean. Enjoy your trip back and the promise of verse 19.

DECEMBER 6   Read Matthew 18:6

When you see a child today, imagine that he or she is Jesus. Thinking of Jesus' own compassion for children, act accordingly. If you don't see any children, think of one for whom you can pray in a special way, or to whom you can send a small gift.

DECEMBER 7   Read Psalm 146

Make a list of those things which you most value, that are included in verse 6—what God has made in the heaven, earth, and sea. Let it become your prayer of thanksgiving to your God of compassion.

DECEMBER 8   Read Zechariah 10:6-12

Substitute your name for "Judah" and "Joseph" in verse 6. Receive this passage as though you could hear God telling it about you and your family to one of your friends.

DECEMBER 9   Read Jonah 3 and 4

What part of the world do you have a hard time thinking of as the object of God's compassion as Jonah did with the Ninevites? Pray that God's great compassion will grow ever stronger within you.

Prince of Peace

*T*is the season to be jolly and saturated with a peace-filled energy that helps me enjoy Christmas to its fullest! So what can I do with those sleepless nights when my body is exhausted but my mind won't shut off? I finally fall into a restless sleep, only to find myself wide awake a few hours later, rehearsing all the details of what needs to be done yet before Christmas Day. Making nocturnal lists doesn't get the jobs done; instead, it wears me out further, antagonizing my senses. What happened to the peace of Christmas?

When my inner peace seems as illusive as peace in the world around me, I have found a meditation that provides some help. You may want to try it. Close your eyes and lie in a comfortable position. Imagine you are on a beach. Feel the sun penetrating your entire body with warmth. Relax your muscles and then melt cozily into the sand. Listen to the pounding of the surf, constant in its rhythmic tide. Let it become God's peace, which is always at the ocean, inviting you to let it soak into your being.

Then imagine the warm water of the breakers, lapping closer to you until it kisses your feet. As it comes again, let it bring that gift of peace to your tired legs and let it drag your busy thoughts back out to sea. Feel it returning for more of your thoughts, rising further and further onto your body until it gently covers all of you in its ebb and flow. Take a deep breath and realize that you can breathe even as this special water of peace covers your face. Let your muscles and mind begin to empty and be lulled to sleep in these loving arms of God's love. Receive the gift God prepared for you in the Prince of Peace.

DECEMBER 10   Read Psalm 29

Experience the Prince of Peace you are given as a blessing by trying
the meditation described on page 170. If you are not ready to sleep,
sit in a comfortable chair instead of lying down. Allow God's peace
to enter and consume you in preparation for the day ahead.

DECEMBER 11   Read Zechariah 9:9, 10

How can you feel God's peace most easily today—through loud
rejoicing or by humbly riding the donkey? Take a few moments
to think about the constancy of the ocean and God's dominion
over all of life, from sea to sea. Let God's peace receive your day.

DECEMBER 12   Read Isaiah 11:1-9

God's perfect kingdom is depicted here being led by a child. List
qualities of your childhood that you can use as a leader in bringing
God's peace to the world today and in the future. Ask for God's
help in preserving that part of you.

DECEMBER 13   Read Psalm 122

Think of your body as the house of God, standing beside the
ocean. For a few minutes, let the roar of the waves drown out

the roar of your plans for the day ahead. Let them bring to you the promise of verse 8, over and over, "Peace be within you."

DECEMBER 14   Read Matthew 5:9

Imagine the peace of Christ that you have experienced this week lapping like the surf around the feet of those with whom you interact today. Plan a specific act or word of peace for at least one person.

DECEMBER 15   Read Isaiah 9:1-7

Pray for the world, that the promise of endless and growing peace, which the Prince of Peace came to bestow, will be known as far and wide and deeply as the waters of the sea.

DECEMBER 16   Read Ephesians 2:11-18

What friend do you think of as being an ocean apart from you in beliefs, experiences, or physical distance? Thank God for the gift of Christ's reconciling peace. Ask for that peace to fill yourself as a way of taking a step toward closing the distance.

Love

"What do you want?" That familiar question comes from parents, grandparents, aunts, uncles, and friends, who are all making their Christmas lists and want to know what we want, as well. Every store and television show, with its Santa Claus figure, visions of lollipops, and everything else imaginable, tries to convince us all that we can have whatever we want.

A commercial this year pictures a small girl climbing onto Santa Claus' lap and bringing him a handful of candy. His heart is melted by this unique little one who seems more interested in giving than receiving. Just as he sits back to enjoy the treat, she says, "Now Santa, about my list...," and a long strip of paper containing her wish list unrolls from her tiny fist, stretching across the floor in front of them.

I am tempted to laugh at this child until I realize that I understand the scene, not only because of watching children, but because of my own tendencies as well. In my prayers I often offer God a handful of praise before I unroll my list of wants. Usually I fail to distinguish between my wants and my needs. And then I wonder why God does not give me what I want!

When I think, however, of God as love, I stop picturing God as a glorified Santa who only gives me what I want. God's love, as broad and deep as the sea, knows me well enough to respond to something more essential and valuable—my needs.

In this busy season of the year, trade the time you have spent worrying about your desires to spending time deliberately trusting God to take care of your needs. Believe that God's immense love is not only a cliché of the season, but a reality which you have been given.

DECEMBER 17   Read Psalm 36:5-7

The truth of God's love can be as overwhelming as the endless ocean. Be still and receive as much of this immense love as you can fathom. Wrap yourself in a big warm blanket as you imagine God's love surrounding you, holding you, and seeping all the way into the core of your soul.

DECEMBER 18   Read Song of Solomon 8:6, 7

Write a love letter to the one who loves you more than any other, through whom you have known more fully the love of God.

DECEMBER 19   Read John 15:9-17

In the love and joy of Christ, plan a gift for someone you know who cannot give in return. If possible, give it anonymously, just as Jesus often gives His love.

DECEMBER 20   Read Romans 12:9-21

Which phrase seems to jump out at you, calling for more attention? Stay with it, and ask God to show you what more you could learn today about how to live this true love.

DECEMBER 21   **Read Proverbs 25:21-22**

Heaping coals of fire on another's head was a gift to the one whose fire had gone out. She would carry it home in a traditional basket on her head to rekindle her fire for cooking and heating. On whose head can you heap coals of fire to rekindle the warmth of God's love, even if it is that person's fault that the fire went out?

DECEMBER 22   **Read Mark 12:28-31**

Express your obedience to the first commandment in a love letter to Jesus—either the baby, the adult, or the Christ. Keep it in your journal.

DECEMBER 23   **Read I Corinthians 13**

Imagine sitting safely in a boat in the middle of a body of water with no land in sight. Let the water turn into God's love, surrounding and upholding you. All you can see is only the beginning of the love God has for you, which never ends. When you are saturated by this complete love, let your boat land. Take part of this love with you today to pour onto another.

DECEMBER 24   Read I John 4:7-21

Close your eyes and relax your body as you listen to the roar of the sea in your imagination. Allow yourself time to be immersed in God's love in the miracle of Jesus' birth which you continue to anticipate. Offer yourself to God as a place in which Jesus' love can be born anew, dwell, and be perfected.

Everlasting

*L*ooking out across the ocean, I laughed with delight as I watched dolphins, two or three at a time, jumping out of the icy winter water. They seemed to be having a big party, flying in and out of the waves as they swam past the beach on which I stood. I envied their carefree life. They were lovely as they went about doing what they were created to do!

Another part of me, however, felt sorry for them and all that they miss in life because they are only dolphins. They can't look forward to seeing their relatives at Christmas. They don't know the joy of giving gifts to their friends. They simply cannot fully know in a personal way the One who created them.

Then I thought about one of my friends who is a child of God, but who grew up without knowing it, almost like the dolphins. The children at school made fun of her, and her parents yelled at her. She had never been told she was loved, so she figured she was a bad person and not worth loving.

Then one day a new family moved next door to her and she soon noticed they were different from the other people she knew. They were kind to her and made her feel special. When they told her God loved her, it began to make sense. After being loved by some of God's children, she could understand that God could love her, too.

The easiest way to know the Lord is with you, just as the angel proclaimed to Mary, is when other Christians show God's love to you. The easiest way for your friends to know the Lord is with them is for you to show God's love to them. Begin with the Christmas event, but continue on as God does, always demonstrating everlasting love.

DECEMBER 25   Read Psalm 93

On this day of celebrating Jesus' birth, relax. Let some of the joy of this event swirl around you. Let the activity of the season be like distant waves crashing on the shore, but for this short time let only the assurance of Jesus' everlasting presence come into your inner being.

DECEMBER 26   Read Luke 2:15-21

Imagine yourself to be Mary in this story. Treasure your place in the event of Jesus' birth and the words of those who come to admire and worship the child who is part of you. Ponder the promise of this Jesus, who will be a part of you forever.

DECEMBER 27   Read Matthew 2:1-15

Write a prayer of confession for the times in the past year when, like Herod, you blocked the working of Jesus in your life. Then let Jesus remind you of the times when, like the Magi, you helped preserve the name of Jesus by your prayers and actions in God's everlasting kingdom.

DECEMBER 28   Read Zechariah 14:6-11

Has this predicted kingdom of God's everlasting reign already begun to flow with living water in your life? Think of a life-giving activity to do today with your family or a friend—something that helps you feel more alive!

DECEMBER 29   Read Ephesians 4:1-16

Look back over the past year and recall the kind of time it was. Was it a year of being tossed around on every wave of the sea, one of resting in calm waters, one of tears, one of bursting with the moving waters of joy? Write a thank you letter to Jesus for the part you have been given to live in the everlasting kingdom of God.

DECEMBER 30   Read Revelation 5

Join the angels in their songs of verses 12 and 13. Look back through the year at those attributes of God of which you have become most aware. Journal about the one that has held the most meaning for you.

DECEMBER 31   Read Ecclesiastes 1:2-7

Think back over your year: the roles you have lived, your accomplishments, your relationships with God and with people. This is the end of a year. It is also the beginning of another year—like the sun seems to circle us each day, like the wind blows around the world, like the cycle of water with streams running to the oceans that are never full. Thank God for allowing you to live in this everlasting cycle, at one with the Everlasting One.

About the Author

Sandra Drescher-Lehman enjoys being a wife to John and mother to Maria and Jonathan. After serving as a prison chaplain for ten years, she is now a social worker in the field of mental health. Her family attends First Mennonite Church in Richmond, Virginia where she coordinates worship. Her greatest challenge is to find the best balance between busyness and being still.